INDONESIA'S TECHNOLOGY STARTUPS
VOICES FROM THE ECOSYSTEM

Palmira Permata Bachtiar, Hening Wikan Sawiji,
Adinda Angelica, Faiq Yahya, and Paul Vandenberg

JUNE 2023

Country Report No. 8
Ecosystems for Technology Startups in Asia and the Pacific

ADB

ASIAN DEVELOPMENT BANK

ISBN 978-92-9270-158-1 (print); 978-92-9270-159-8 (electronic); 978-92-9270-160-4 (ebook)
Publication Stock No. TCS230176-2
DOI: http://dx.doi.org/10.22617/TCS230176-2

The views expressed in this publication are those of the authors and do not necessarily reflect the views and policies of the Asian Development Bank (ADB) or its Board of Governors or the governments they represent.

ADB does not guarantee the accuracy of the data included in this publication and accepts no responsibility for any consequence of their use. The mention of specific companies or products of manufacturers does not imply that they are endorsed or recommended by ADB in preference to others of a similar nature that are not mentioned.

By making any designation of or reference to a particular territory or geographic area, or by using the term "country" in this publication, ADB does not intend to make any judgments as to the legal or other status of any territory or area.

Corrigenda to ADB publications may be found at http://www.adb.org/publications/corrigenda.

Note:
In this publication, "$" refers to United States dollars, "Rp" refers to rupiah, and "S$" refers to Singapore dollars. ADB recognizes "China" as the People's Republic of China.

All photos are owned by ADB unless otherwise stated.

Cover design by Joe Mark Ganaban.

Contents

Tables, Figures, and Boxes

Foreword

New business models continue to disrupt the global economy, spurred by new technologies and their use in providing goods and services in innovative ways. Indonesia's growing list of unicorns —Gojek, Bukalapak, Ovo, Tokopedia, J&T Express, and others—are part of this disruption. Indonesians can now order food, hail a taxi, move money, arrange travel, watch entertainment, shop for most things, and even consult a doctor or take courses using digital methods. At a deeper level, technology is affecting production processes in the form of Industry 4.0. Technology-based startup enterprises—or tech startups, for short—are an important part of the evolving business-to-business and business-to-consumer landscape in in Indonesia and around the world.

Startups develop in an ecosystem that can support—or hinder—their development. Indonesia's ecosystem involves many national elements, but regional and international factors also are important, especially in its increasingly open and globalized economy. Finance, often from venture capital, and skilled personnel are important parts of the ecosystem. Good digital infrastructure and supportive government policy are also critical. Startups develop best when the markets for their goods and services are large and active.

This report analyzes Indonesia's ecosystem and assesses the support it gives to the growing number of startups. The report focuses on the country's startups in four areas: agritech, edtech, healthtech, and greentech (also known as cleantech). These four areas not only contribute to economic activity but can have a deeper impact on socioeconomic development. Edtech and healthtech contribute to human capital formation while agritech improves productivity and raises incomes in the rural sector where many of the poor people work. Greentech advances environmental sustainability and climate change mitigation.

The analysis of Indonesia's ecosystem provides recommendations for policy makers both in Indonesia and other countries in Southeast Asia. My hope is that high-quality ecosystems can better support startups throughout the Asia and Pacific region.

Albert Park
Chief Economist
Asian Development Bank

Acknowledgments

The report was prepared by the SMERU Research Institute and the Asian Development Bank (ADB). Key contributors for SMERU are Palmira Permata Bachtiar, Hening Wikan Sawiji, Adinda Angelica, Faiq Yahya; and for ADB, Paul Vandenberg. Aimee Hampel-Milagrosa provided guidance on study design and Rana Hasan and Lei Lei Song offered management support.

ADB's Indonesia Resident Mission reviewed the report and helped solicit comments from the Government of Indonesia. The authors would like to thank key experts from government, incubators, accelerators, development partners, investors, academic institutions, and startups who provided invaluable insights to researchers that were used in the preparation of this study. The draft report was reviewed by the Center for Macroeconomic Policy, Fiscal Policy Agency, Ministry of Finance, Indonesia.

Tuesday Soriano copyedited the report, and Amanda Isabel Mamon provided administrative support, contracting, and manuscript management.

Abbreviations

ADB	Asian Development Bank
Amvesindo	Asosiasi Modal Ventura dan Startup Indonesia (Indonesian Association of Venture Capital and Startups)
B2B	business to business
B2C	business to consumer
BRIN	Badan Riset dan Inovasi Nasional (National Research and Innovation Agency)
COVID-19	coronavirus disease
CPPBT	Calon Perusahaan Pemula Berbasis Teknologi (Tech-Based Pre-Startup Grant Program)
CVC	corporate venture capital
ECF	equity crowdfunding
IPO	initial public offering
Kemenkominfo	Kementerian Komunikasi dan Informatika (Ministry of Communication and Information Technology)
KPI	key performance indicator
KUR	Kredit Usaha Rakyat (Small-Scale Credit Program)
OJK	Otoritas Jasa Keuangan (Financial Services Authority)
PPBR	Perusahaan Pemula Berbasis Riset (Research-Based Startups)
PPBT	Perusahaan Pemula Berbasis Teknologi (Tech-Based Startup Grant Program)
R&D	research and development
RPJMN	Rencana Pembangunan Jangka Menengah Nasional (National Medium-Term Development Plan)
SDGs	Sustainable Development Goals
SMEs	small and medium-sized enterprises
SoE	state-owned enterprise
VC	venture capital

Executive Summary

Overview

Tech startups require an ecosystem of support that differs from the assistance provided to traditional small enterprises. The ecosystem should comprise not only dedicated government policies and programs, but also financing solutions, support from incubator and accelerator programs, and talent development (human resources) versed in technological innovation, but also in inventing new business models. The ecosystem includes public, private, and quasi-public players. Building this ecosystem is critical to developing a vibrant community of tech startups.

Indonesia has established an ecosystem for tech startups. Most of the components have been put in place in the last 5 years, which is a similar time frame to other countries in the region. The challenge now is to deepen this support by understanding what works best and adjusting and refining the measures. There are lessons to be learned from other countries, notably Singapore, which attracts many startups because of its supportive ecosystem.

Better geographic distribution of support would be helpful. Key ecosystem players and programs are concentrated in Java and Bali, while other areas are underserviced. It is useful to move away from thinking of one national ecosystem and instead consider multiple city and local ecosystems that service proximate clients (startups). Globally, ecosystems are most often organized (and assessed) at the city or local level (e.g., Silicon Valley).

Three key areas for improvement are the quality of incubators and accelerators, financial access for early-stage startups, and talent development. These three areas were identified as needing improvement to better support startups. Incubators and accelerators would benefit from improved staffing (i.e., employees with more business knowledge) and mentors with sector expertise and experience. It is a challenge to find good talent because of the short supply and competition from large firms in hiring the best and brightest. Early-stage startups find it difficult to convince equity investors to provide funding, and alternative sources may need to be developed.

Startups in development-oriented sectors face specific challenges. Startups engaged in agritech, edtech, healthtech, and greentech (also known as cleantech) generate both economic and developmental benefits. Tech innovations in education and health improve human capital and well-being. Agriculture employs a large share of the poor population. Greentech provides solutions to combat environmental degradation and climate change. These areas are often seen as risky, and investors lack knowledge about them compared with the popular fintech and e-commerce sectors. Dedicated support to these four sectors is needed.

Incubators and Accelerators

The number and variety of incubator and accelerator programs has grown in the last 5 years. There are four types, based on sponsorship or ownership: (i) publicly sponsored, (ii) nonprofit, (iii) private university, and (iv) privately sponsored. Publicly sponsored programs are provided by sector-based research and development centers of the central government, sectoral agencies of local government, and state universities. Most programs provide support in the areas of business management, legal advice, technology, and marketing. Programs are funded in various ways and from various sources that include internally generated funds, funds from networks, government funds, and funds from partnerships with corporations.

Programs are concentrated in the large cities. About 60% of all incubator and accelerator programs are in Java. Other areas are not as well serviced, and startups outside of Java find it more challenging to join a program.

Most incubators and accelerators view themselves as effective in supporting their tenants. They also feel that there are sufficient programs in Java to support the startup community. However, they recognize that some perform less well than others and that management in some programs is weak. They also recognize the lack of adequate geographic coverage across the country. Financing institutions that operate their own incubator and accelerator programs tend to view the programs as effective, although less important than financing. However, financial institutions that do not have their own programs tend to view them as mostly ineffective.

The quality of incubators and accelerators is a concern. Many programs have limited management capacity, lack dedicated full-time staff, and have not established standard operating procedures. Some programs lack sustained funding, and others have only a limited network with other players in the ecosystem. Local government incubators are often managed by government staff who have limited understanding of the business world and how startups are run. The private sector finds it difficult to operate incubators on a profitable basis. In addition, the inability to identify suitable mentors who can provide quality, sector-specific mentorship is also a constraint. Creating networks with other players in the ecosystem is an unfulfilled priority.

Programs face an uphill battle in assembling a competent management team. The challenge varies depending on the type of incubator or accelerator. Publicly sponsored programs lack business professionals on their teams. They are also expected to become the source of grants in the ecosystem. Government agencies feel that nonprofit programs treat tech startups the same as small and medium-sized enterprises and therefore do not provide the targeted assistance that startups need. University incubator and accelerator programs also lack business professionals and financial resources.

Programs face funding challenges. Government funds can only be used to directly provide assistance for startups, leaving incubators and accelerators without sufficient funds to cover the costs of their facilities and services. Meanwhile, privately sponsored programs have difficulty in generating funds, especially those that are not directly linked to venture capital and corporate venture capital. Many programs have had their operations limited by the lockdown restrictions imposed as a result of the coronavirus disease (COVID-19) pandemic.

Financing Institutions

Both the supply and demand for startup funding continue to grow—but a gap remains. Startups can tap into various financing sources, from individual savings to institutional sources. Angel investment and venture capital (independent and corporate, local and foreign) are available, as are less commonly used crowdfunding platforms and banks. Some incubators and accelerators also offer funding. The number of financing institutions supporting startups has increased to about 200. Considering its market size, Indonesia is a promising location for foreign startup investors. Since a majority of Indonesia's commercial activity is concentrated in Jakarta and the Java-Bali region, capital is unequally spread.

Traditional financial institutions, like banks, are a limited source of finance for startups. A key constraint is that early-stage startups are not able to furnish the necessary documents such as a balance sheet or income statement. They are unable to show a revenue flow—because at the early stage they have little revenue—and therefore would have difficulty servicing credit.

Angel investors and venture capitalists are important partners for startups. Along with finance, they often offer strategic guidance on technology and business management and provide access to networks. Angel investors are sought after because they invest at the early stage (when the risk of failure is high) and their decision-making is faster than venture capital funds. However, the number of angel investors is very limited. Singapore and the Republic of Korea are good practice cases where the government provides matching funds once the startup receives funding from financial institutions or businesses.

Funding is scarce at the early stages. There might be more angel investors to provide funding in the development stage. Investors have different criteria and assess startups differently based on their stage of development and sector. The degree of product-market fit is an important criterion to access funding, which startups often struggle to meet.

Not all startups want to obtain equity funding. Early-stage startups often avoid seeking equity investment because they fear losing control of the enterprise. Some startups would rather take out a loan, especially to finance working capital.

Access to finance differs among the four sectors studied. There is limited access to finance for cleantech startups. Investors are reluctant to invest in cleantech and agritech because the business model is capital intensive and offers riskier deep-tech solutions. There are big players in edtech and a major player in agritech, which may be paving the way for growing interest in these sectors. Nevertheless, there is a large funding gap in all four sectors.

Internal and External Success Factors

Four internal processes determine the success of a startup. They are (i) idea generation—or problem validation; (ii) market validation; (iii) business model; and (iv) competitiveness. Most startups fail because the idea lacks originality and is only a slight modification of an existing product or service with little added value. Even if the idea is brilliant, it still needs to be validated—it must solve a real problem facing consumers or other businesses. The idea must be implemented through an appropriate business model. And finally, the product should clearly stand out from competing products and be difficult to copy.

While the idea is important, the execution of a good idea is even more important. Founders must have a clear and original vision and not just follow the trend. Founders should have a common vision, otherwise conflict will arise. A shared vision makes for a solid team. Its absence makes it almost impossible to execute a brilliant idea. The character of the founders is crucial to maintain a solid team. For financing institutions, the team is often more important than the product. An ideal team is composed of members with different skills that complement each other. A team that excels only in inventing and is weak in marketing is prone to fail. Management skills are also essential. Startups need to manage their cash flow wisely. Once they run out of cash, friction will arise. And finally, an entrepreneurial mindset is needed, which is unfortunately often lacking in startups.

The government has created a variety of support programs over the past 5 years. With the exception of the Tech-Based Startup Grant Program and the Tech-Based Pre-Startup Grant Program, which finance startup development through incubators, the other government programs are generally perceived to focus on raising awareness, nurturing enthusiasm, and encouraging youth participation. In other words, they are good for promotional purposes. Moreover, government programs are often not sustainable and are administratively burdensome for startups because of the considerable application and compliance paperwork. Compliance targets are sometimes unreasonably high.

Three important external factors for startups are the pandemic, talent, and timing. First, many startups terminated their operations due to the pandemic. However, there are also startups whose growth was boosted by the pandemic. Second, the talent deficit is often cited as an important constraint for startups. Investors will only come to Indonesia—attracted by the size of the market— if talent (i.e., trained and skilled human resources) is there to execute startups' ideas. Unicorns (and large traditional companies) seek to hire the same talent as startups, and they have a hard time competing for engineers, programmers, designers, and others. Finally, timing—despite being rarely mentioned—is in fact a very important factor. A product may be validated to solve a problem, but if the market is not ready at the time, the startup will not succeed.

Support at Different Stages of the Life Cycle

In the formation stage, startups need to formulate a business model, build a team, and advance the technology. Support needed at this stage includes business support, technology assistance, legal assistance, and marketing assistance. Business assistance refers to business knowledge, the business model, and team management. Technology assistance includes product or service refinement and prototyping. Legal assistance includes certification and legalization of the new product. And market assistance includes market identification, demand, and pricing.

In the stability stage, the key challenges are product refinement and building a network for collaboration. The product needs to be fully developed, finalized, and validated by the market. Business management advice remains a critical factor as the team develops and the business model is solidified. Funding becomes increasingly important to fully produce, launch, and market the product. Legal support includes knowledge of and compliance with government rules. Marketing support includes opportunities to work with external parties.

In the scaling stage, funding is a main concern. Funds are needed to scale up output to reach more customers. This means expanding the team (hiring), ramping up production of a physical product, and ensuring sufficient back-up capacity if the product is a digital or platform-based service. Business support in this stage includes mentoring for financial management as revenues increase and cost control becomes important.

Agritech

Agritech startups noted the importance of government programs, particularly at the early stage. Programs that educate farmers about the benefits of technology open the market for agritech startups. The government is essential to execute support programs and create an enabling environment by designing policies and regulations to improve the ecosystem. However, some government programs supporting startups have high application and compliance costs (i.e., paperwork).

Understanding the market is critical. The product must fit the needs of the market, and founders need to know that market through research, analysis, and networking with farmers and other industry players. Incubators and accelerators are important to provide professional mentors, open access to investors and the market, and create a network to share knowledge and problems. Foreign investors can open access to "go international."

Agritech startups face the digital divide and mistrust of new brands or products. Consumer (farmer) education is particularly important in the context of the digital divide. Digital products and services require farmers to have some level of digital literacy. Also, the Indonesian market is characterized by low trust in new products and brands. Established suppliers are preventing newcomers from entering the market for agricultural inputs and services.

Edtech

Financing institutions lack interest in the education sector. Venture capitalists are more interested in e-commerce and fintech, where revenue and profits can be generated more quickly. Edtech startups require more time to show promising results. Moreover, investors are mostly interested in funding potential unicorns rather than early-stage startups. The education sector, in particular, has long been on the negative list for investment and thus has not received foreign investment, although restrictions have recently been eased. Greater support for edtech startups to access investment funding would be beneficial.

Trust and demand need to be developed. Edtech startups struggle to gain the trust of people. However, the coronavirus disease (COVID-19) pandemic has expanded the market and demand for edtech, which should create momentum for startups' products among consumers and the government. The employment training support program, Kartu Prakerja, has helped increase demand for edtech.

Important internal factors are the founder, the team, and the product. Investors are interested in founders with strong leadership skills. Selecting team members with the same vision and close cohesion is important considering that they will be working together for a long time. In terms of product, many startups do not develop an original product. Instead, they try to modify products from other countries, only to find that they cannot be used in Indonesia.

Partnerships and networking can be improved. In addition to the issues noted above, startups could benefit from support that helps them foster business partnerships and improve networking with investors.

Healthtech

The market for many healthtech innovations comprises health-care providers (e.g., hospitals, clinics, etc.). This requires a different marketing approach than if the clients are individuals. Attracting these providers as customers is a key challenge for startups, in part due to the competition they face from large, established suppliers.

Health is a sensitive area, and startups need to navigate health regulations. Product safety and effectiveness are critical elements that need to be tested and certified. Therefore, startups in this sector need to invest in their own testing and be able to demonstrate results to regulators and customers. Some digital innovations from startups are helping to improve the management of patient records, which involve sensitive issues of privacy and confidentiality.

Expanding mentorship and creating regulatory sandboxes are important support activities. Mentors with sector experience and knowledge of the medical field are in short supply, but they are critical to understanding the needs of healthtech startups and designing solutions for them. Furthermore, regulations may not exist for new innovations, or regulations may be obsolete. Creating regulatory sandboxes will allow the government to experiment with startups and develop agile regulations.

Cleantech

Incubator and accelerator programs are helpful for startups—but there are caveats. Programs are spread across the country, which is good, but the effectiveness of some programs is low and there is a lack of continuity and follow-up after graduation from a program. Cleantech-focused programs and mentors are in short supply.

Funding for cleantech startups and the environment sector is limited. The sector is still seen as relatively unattractive and risky. This is partly because the market is seen as small. Startups find that fundraising is difficult because of limited access to financiers, lack of knowledge about investment criteria, and difficulty agreeing on terms for a deal.

In the formation stage, the most significant challenge is product development. Experiments and the iteration of ideas are commonplace, making research and development capacity and resources particularly important.

Recruiting highly skilled talent is a significant challenge. Cleantech talent is scarce, expensive, and in high demand at large tech-based enterprises (i.e., often "graduated" startups) and traditional corporations. Attracting talent may require showing them the excitement, freedom to innovate, and opportunity to be part of something truly game-changing that startups can offer.

The "rules of the game" for the cleantech sector are unclear. Government regulations are still lacking in certain areas, creating uncertainty for startups and their potential clients (e.g., what equipment and processes are needed to meet regulatory standards). However, some startups benefit from the gray area created by uncertain or unregulated areas.

Advocates of environmental protection play a key role in the sector. They raise awareness of the need to address climate change and therefore help to grow the market for cleantech solutions. Science-related problems require science-based solutions.

Introduction

Along with the expansion of digital technology, the past 2 decades have witnessed the rise of a new type of business entity—the startup. It is not merely a business that starts up, but one that possesses an innovative technology—or uses an existing technology in an innovative way—and is delivered through a unique business model. Because many startups harness the power of the internet, they can rapidly scale their operations to reach thousands or millions of potential customers. Innovative technology, business model, and scalability are thus the defining characteristics of startups.

Startups start small, but they are inherently different from traditional small and medium-sized enterprises (SMEs). They differ in innovation and technology, but also in other areas. Hecht (2017) suggests that the differences can be seen in their growth purpose, method of funding, and final goal. The purpose of an SME is to make profit from serving the market efficiently. Funding is provided through bank loans, and the end goal is to build a self-sustaining and long-lasting business. A startup, on the other hand, seeks to disrupt the market with a new technology and business model. It is funded by venture capital, with investors taking a share of ownership. The end vision of startups is either an initial public offering (IPO) or sale and takeover by another, larger company.[1]

Businesses that began as tech startups are now some of the largest companies in the world—Google, Facebook, Amazon, and Alibaba. These companies generate enormous value for the economies in which they are located. They disrupt markets and employment, and cause the creative destruction of other enterprises, but they make a net positive contribution. For these reasons, cities and countries around the world want to nurture, foster, and encourage the establishment and growth of startups. They are doing so by creating a new branch of enterprise support.

---

[1] There are different types of startups. Some are software (digital) startups and others are deep tech. The latter develop more complex technology and include robotics, synthetic biology, and advanced materials (Wang 2021). Deep tech startups are considered the fourth wave of innovation after the third wave of digitalization (Rosenberg 2021). Deep tech startups use software extensively, but their success depends on creating hardware. They face greater technology risk than market risk and their problems are very different from e-commerce.

In addition to traditional efforts to encourage the growth of microenterprises and SMEs, governments are enacting policies and setting up dedicated programs to nurture startups.

However, it is now widely recognized that government is only one factor influencing the success of startups. Other players, institutions, and elements are also important, such as financiers, digital infrastructure, and incubators and accelerators. Markets are also critical, including suppliers of inputs and, of course, demand from customers who buy the output. Another key element is the supply of talent—tech, entrepreneurial, and otherwise. Mentors who provide guidance and a culture that encourages risk-taking are other supporting factors. Together, they comprise the startup ecosystem (Figure 1). Building a complete, deep, and integrated ecosystem is the best way to ensure that more startups are established and that they can sustain and scale their operations. This report examines the startup ecosystem in Indonesia.

Figure 1: Tech Startups Ecosystem

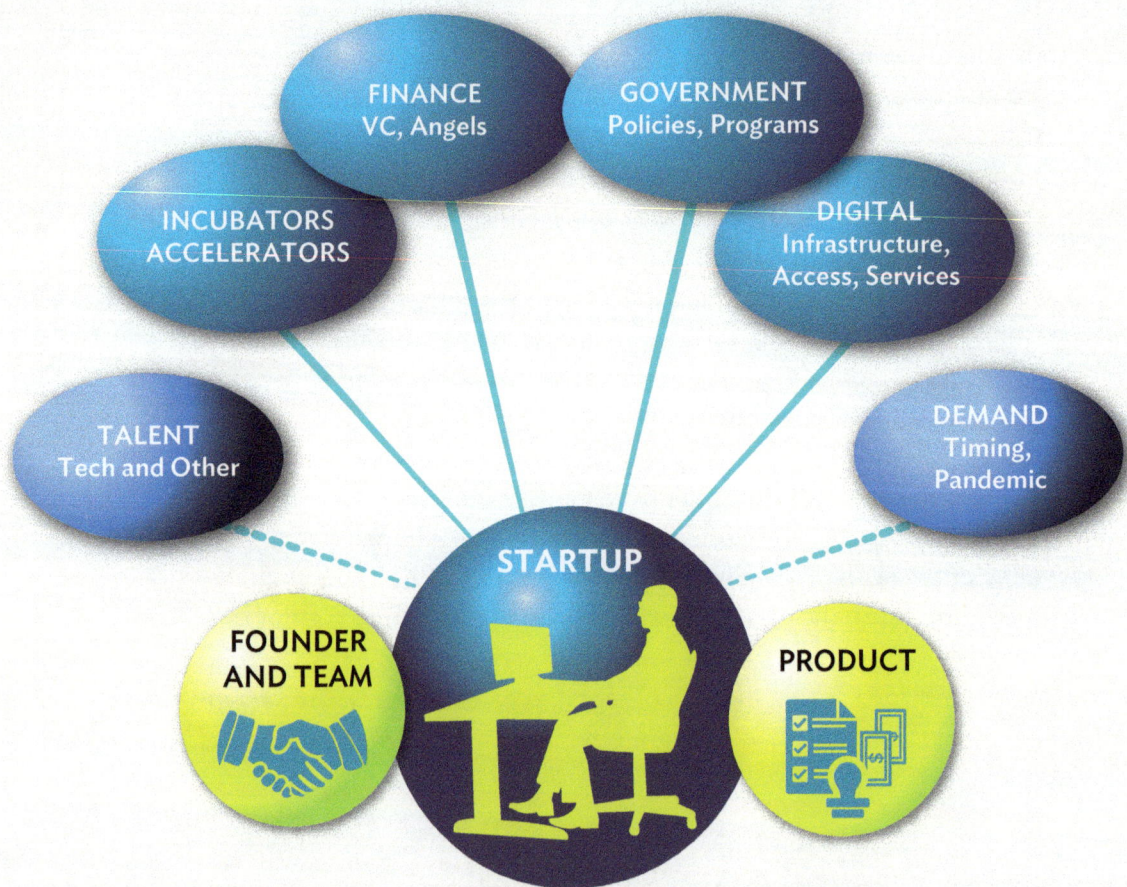

VC = venture capital.
Source: Authors.

1.1 Startups in Indonesia

Startups began to emerge in the 2000s, and the following decade saw a rapid increase in their number. The year 2010 was a watershed year, with the establishment of the Indonesian Association of Venture Capital and Startups (Amvesindo) and two key funding transactions: East Venture invested in Tokopedia, a future unicorn, and PT Telkom funded Plasa.com, now Belanja.com (Manurung 2018). Several new venture capital (VC) firms were established the following year, and Indonesia's ecosystem gained greater maturity in 2014 when a Singaporean funder provided capital for Gojek, which helped it become the country's first unicorn 2 years later. Since then, the number of startups has steadily increased to reach 2,431 by 2022— second only to India among Asian economies. There are also now 12 unicorns and 1 decacorn (Rayda 2022).[2]

The increase in startups has been aided by the development of the ecosystem. There are now about 120 incubators and accelerators in Indonesia, as well as 200 financing institutions that cater wholly or partially to startups. Digital infrastructure is improving, and the population is becoming more accustomed to buying products and services online offered by or through startups. Governments at the national and city levels have played a role in introducing programs for startups and incubator programs to support them. There is a buzz about startups that did not exist 10 years ago, and they have become part of the business and consumer culture. Jakarta currently ranks 52nd among city ecosystems in the world and second in Southeast Asia. It is ranked 22nd among emerging ecosystems (city and/or country).

Despite the progress, Indonesia's ecosystem is not yet complete and fully functional, and the startup community continues to evolve. Most startups do not advance beyond the early stage of development and face challenges of sustainability and scalability. They enter the "valley of death"—a high-risk period in which they try to reach scale in an environment of competition, uncertainty, and creative disruption. Some survive the valley; others succumb to it. The coronavirus virus disease (COVID-19) pandemic in 2020–2023 dampened demand for many startups, and the number of failures increased (although others seized the opportunity to expand or pivot by offering remote access to goods and services).

The ecosystem continues to have its weaknesses. Funding is scarce in the early stages, and more angel investment could be encouraged. The number of incubators and accelerators has increased, but the quality of some of them remains questionable, especially in providing sector-specific and real-world business advice. More experienced mentors are needed to guide startups in their early and growth stages. Funding and support are spread unequally across the country,

---

[2]   Startup Ranking. Countries with the Top Startups Worldwide.

with startups in Java and Bali having access to good support, while those in other regions are not as well serviced. Digital infrastructure also needs to be improved to increase internet speeds and expand coverage of high-quality services beyond the major cities. These and other concerns are identified and discussed in the report, and recommendations are made on how to address them.

1.2 Four Sectors for Human and Sustainable Development

Most startups are in the fintech and e-commerce market segments. Other segments attract fewer startups, but they can not only impact economic activity but also support human and sustainable development. This report focuses on four of these sectors: agritech, edtech, greentech, and healthtech (Table 1). Startups in agriculture can help improve productivity and yields, thereby raising incomes for often poor farm households. In education, startups can improve teaching and learning, and thus human capital development. Greentech startups help improve the physical environment and mitigate climate change. Greentech includes both support for the development of cleaner energy and efforts to clean up the environment, such as cleaning up solid and liquid waste and emissions. Startups in health develop solutions for improved curative and preventive health care, enhancing human life and human capital.

Table 1: Four Sectors of Tech Startups and the Sustainable Development Goals

Sector	Innovations Offered by Tech Startups	Sustainable Development Goals
Agritech	• Tech solutions for smart farms • Smart irrigations, crop monitoring • Automation of farming practices • Use of drones	Goal 2: Zero hunger
Cleantech	• Sustainable energy (i.e., solar, wind) • Tech for reduce, recycle, and reuse • Cleaning air and water discharge	Goal 6: Clean water and sanitation Goal 7: Affordable and clean energy
Edtech	• In-school teaching solutions • Attendance monitoring and administration • After-school tutoring apps • School, program, scholarship search • Grading and feedback mechanisms • AR, VR for teaching	Goal 4: Quality of education
Healthtech	• Tech for improved health treatment within hospitals and clinics • For diagnosis, prescription, treatment, and monitoring outside of hospitals and clinics	Goal 3: Good health and well-being

AR = augmented reality, VR = virtual reality.
Source: Vandenberg, P., A. Hampel-Milagrosa, and M. Helble. 2020. Financing of Tech Startups in Selected Asian Countries. *ADBI Working Paper Series*. No. 1115. Tokyo: ADB Institute.

These four sectors face different challenges than e-commerce and fintech. First, they may produce physical products that need to be manufactured, rather than soft services delivered over the internet. Therefore, they need product engineers and contract manufacturers, as well as imported components. Greentech is heavily focused on manufacturing physical products. Second, they need more time to develop the product through prototyping and testing. Investors may not have the patience and instead look for faster returns in more common segments. Third, the clientele may be poor and unable to afford the product, and clients may not have the digital access (and literacy) to avail of the service. Fourth, the sector and its technology may be less well known to investors, who may see these segments as riskier and therefore are less willing to provide funding.

Nonetheless, there may be important synergies between fintech and e-commerce on the one hand and these four development-oriented sectors on the other. First, fintech can provide innovative financing to help startups survive and achieve scale. Second, fintech payment services can be used by startups to provide easy payment options for customers. Third, the business models developed by fintech and e-commerce can provide lessons or examples for adoption by the four sectors.

1.3   Methodology

The study is based on interviews with startups and stakeholders. It is also supported by information from published secondary materials (on the nature of startups and ecosystems) and information on tech startups and programs in Indonesia. Interviews were conducted with 39 startup founders (or key team members), 10 managers and staff of incubators and accelerators, 5 government officials involved with startups, 4 financiers, and several others. Interviewees were asked about the effectiveness of ecosystem support, gaps in available support, and challenges startups face. Some of the insights are not about the ecosystem per se, but about internal success (and failure) factors of the startups themselves, such as the founder's vision, the coherence of the core team, and others. Statistical data are provided from external sources. In some places, data are provided from discussions with a number of interviewees. The report, as the reader will see, contains many direct quotes from interviewees.[3]

---

[3]   A similar methodology was used for eight other country reports on startup ecosystems. These reports have been published in a series by the Asian Development Bank (ADB) and can be accessed at ADB. Ecosystems for Technology Startups in Asia and the Pacific.

The interview method has its strengths and weaknesses. Its strength is that it allows active players in the field to express their views and opinions directly. It allows the interviewer and the interviewee to discuss issues in detail and beyond the confines of a questionnaire with a limited number of set responses. Its weakness is the inability to generalize the views expressed to the wider population. Where possible, the study team sought to corroborate the views of the interviewees by checking other sources (published material).

1.4 Guiding Questions and Structure of the Report

This report examines the ecosystem in Indonesia and the support it provides for startups. The study that produced this report sought answers to four broad questions:

- What type of support is provided by the ecosystem?
- What are the strengths and weaknesses of the ecosystem's components?
- What other (internal) factors help or constrain startups?
- What policy recommendations can be made to improve the ecosystem?

These questions relate to the ecosystem in general and the four focused market segments of agritech, edtech, greentech, and healthtech.

After this introduction, the report has three main parts. The first part examines the key components of the ecosystem that affect all startups. It also considers the qualities of a successful founder, the coherence and composition of the core team, and the importance of founder and team attributes to financiers funding decisions. This is followed by a discussion of the stages of startup development and how the importance of each type of support varies by stage. The second part consists of four chapters, one for each of the market segments. Each segment has unique characteristics and faces unique challenges. The third and final part provides policy recommendations.

Key Components and Startup Evolution

2

Startups are supported by the key components of the ecosystem. In contrast, the absence of, weakness in, or lack of access to these components hinders the development of startups. The six key components of the ecosystem are listed in Table 2. The first three—incubators and accelerators, finance, and government programs—are known to be fundamental aspects of the ecosystem. Digital infrastructure is also important because many startup innovations are offered on or accessible through the internet. Digital infrastructure and related digital literacy issues are not discussed in this chapter but are assessed in subsequent sector chapters.

The last two components of the ecosystem are somewhat unique in that they each group together several sub-elements and combine issues that are "out there" in the ecosystem with others that are internal to the startup. These two components are (i) the founder, team, and talent; and (ii) product innovation, market, and timing. These aspects were uncovered during the fieldwork, and although they do not fit neatly into the concept of the ecosystem as a set of factors external to the startup, they are included because they appear to be important in determining startup success.

For analytical purposes, we divide the ecosystem into discrete components. However, it is important to bear in mind that these components are interdependent and overlapping. Incubators can provide mentors and links to financiers. Financiers can provide networks to suppliers and customers. Government can coinvest with venture capitalists, and so on. The ecosystem as a whole is complex, and coordination among players—by design or by chance—can be important.[4]

Finally, we recognize that startups evolve and change, and indeed can scale rapidly. During this evolution, their needs change and so does the support they seek. These are the development or life cycle stages of the startup, and the final part of this chapter maps the stages and the changing nature of the support they need.

---

[4] For a discussion of definitions, components, and interrelatedness in ecosystems, see Hubbub Labs. What Is a Startup Ecosystem and How Can You Build One?; Startup Commons. Starting Point for Ecosystem Development; and Kirk (2021).

The chapter provides general insights that are relevant to all four sectors that are the subject of this study, as well as sectors that are not specifically covered in the study. Subsequent chapters discuss each of the four market segments of agritech, edtech, cleantech, and healthtech, in more detail.

Table 2: Key Components of the Ecosystem

Ecosystem Factor	Dimensions, Type of Support	External or Internal Factor
Incubators and accelerators	• Business assistance and guidance • Strategic direction • Networking opportunities	• External
Finance	• Access to funding • Grant, venture capital (VC), angels, corporate VC, prizes • Advice along with finance	• External • Internal: own funds, financial management
Government	• Support programs • Government as regulator • Providing opportunities (user, buyer)	• External
Digital infrastructure (and literacy)	• Access, coverage • Quality (speed) • Cost (affordability by customers)	• External
Founder(s), team, talent	• Founder's vision • Management team • Founder–team relationship	• Internal: founder, team dynamics • External: securing talent
Demand: product, market, timing (pandemic)	• Product-market fit and validation • Market strategy and marketing • Changing market opportunities • Pandemic pivot	• Internal: product development • External: market, fit, timing

Source: Authors.

2.1   Incubators and Accelerators

Business incubator and accelerator programs offer a range of advisory and support services to get startups established and scaling up. Incubators provide early-stage support that often continues for 2 years. Some incubators provide physical premise for startups, often referred to as coworking space. Accelerators provide higher-level or strategic assistance, usually for 3 to 6 months, that helps more established startups to grow and scale up.[5] Some startups will complete an incubator program and then join an accelerator.

---

[5]   For a discussion of the characteristics and differences of incubators and accelerators, see Wise and Valliere (2014) and Brillyanes and Samira (2019).

There is no standard set of services offered by all incubators or accelerators; each offers its own mix.[6] From interviews conducted for this report, the assistance provided for tech startups in Indonesia can include the following areas:

- Business: advice on strategy, management and operations, provision of coworking space
- Finance: seed capital, links to investors and financial institutions
- Legal: certification of product standards, business registration, regulatory compliance, others
- Technology: advice on product development, technology implementation
- Links to partners: creating networks with suppliers and manufacturing partners
- Marketing: advice and access to the product market and buyers

Programs can be categorized by the nature of their sponsorship. Gozali et al. (2015) suggest that the main sponsor may be the government, a nonprofit organization, a university, or private (large) businesses. These four types are depicted in Table 3, which also indicates the type of the 10 programs whose staff were interviewed for this study.[7] Most of those interviewed were from privately sponsored programs, including all accelerators.[8]

Table 3: Types of Incubator and Accelerator Programs, by Sponsorship

	Public (government)	Nonprofit	University	Private (other businesses)
Nature of the sponsor	Government, including agencies and development commissions	Community organizations and associations	Research departments, mostly in science and technology	Private businesses
Objectives	Private sector development and job creation i.e., reduce unemployment	Area and social development	Commercialize and spin off new research discoveries	Identify investment opportunities, create innovative subsidiaries
Incubators interviewed	IA-1	IA-4, IA-9	IA-3, IA-5	IA-2, IA-6, IA-7, IA-10
Accelerators interviewed	–	–	–	IA-2, IA-6, IA-7, IA-8

IA = incubator or accelerator.
Note: See Appendix for the names of programs at which staff were interviewed.
Source: Authors.

---

[6] For the range of services that can be offered, see Rice (2002), Ratinho and Henriques (2010), Bruneel et al. (2012), and Baraldi and Havenvid (2016).

[7] Three of the programs had an incubator and an accelerator component.

[8] There are some publicly sponsored accelerators, but they were not interviewed.

Figure 2: The Sufficiency and Effectiveness of Incubator or Accelerator Programs in Indonesia

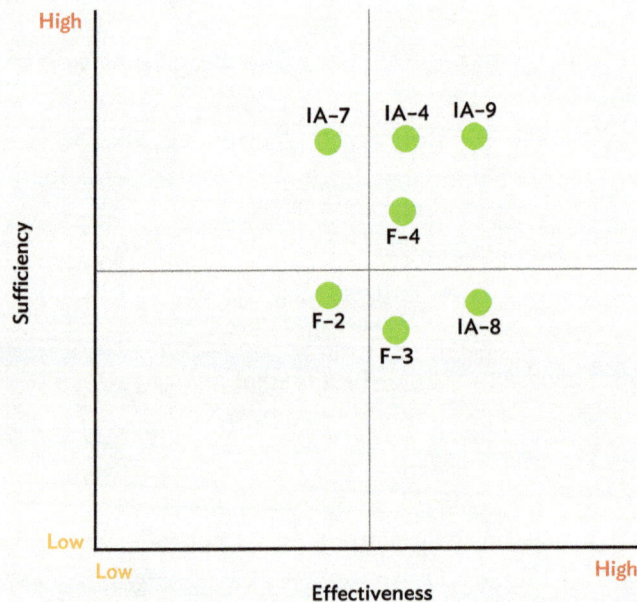

IA = incubator or accelerator, F = financing institution.
Note: The numbers relate to the list of programs in the Appendix.
Source: Authors.

Perception of Financing Institutions on Sufficiency and Effectiveness

To determine whether there are a sufficient number of programs and whether they are effective, we asked four financiers and staff of eight programs for their views. A variety of opinions were expressed and are shown in Figure 2. It should be noted that there were about 120 active programs and 2,200 known startups in 2020, although there are likely many unknown startups just getting started.[9] If we assume that all known startups seek the support of an incubator or accelerator, the ratio is about 18 startups per program.

Of the four financing institutions interviewed, one felt the number of programs was sufficient, two said it was insufficient, and one did not express an opinion. Two financiers felt that the services provided by current programs were not effective in fostering startup growth, while one felt they were effective, and one did not express an opinion.

---

[9] These figures do not indicate the number of startups in programs, only all known startups and programs.

The differences in perspective are related to the interviewee's program affiliation. Those financiers who had an incubator or accelerator program in their network tended to view the programs as effective, even if their role is considered less important than financing. This impression was driven by two main factors. First, financing institutions perceived the programs as a mechanism to de-risk their investments in startups. These programs allow financing institutions to build more awareness and assess in advance the startups in which they might invest. Second, the programs allow financing institutions to nurture potential startups in sectors preferred by financiers. The financing institutions come on board (with financing) once the startup reaches a certain stage of development. A manager of a financing institution highlighted these elements:

> As a venture capitalist, we have been running an accelerator program since 2016 in collaboration with the Australian government. Through this program, we were able to have a better interaction with the startup founders. Therefore, we had a better assessment of their business character followed by us having a list of potential startups to work with (Incubator-Accelerator no. 7).

This approach is common in Indonesia. The privately sponsored incubators and accelerators interviewed positioned their programs as a mechanism for investors (i.e., themselves) to view and filter early-stage startups for potential investment. This is critical because the financier has limited opportunity to evaluate startups at their initial phase. At the same time, the programs boost the startup's capabilities and give it a greater chance of success. As another financier noted,

> We have had a business incubator program since 2017. Most financing institutions do. The incubator program is considered effective in assisting the growth of early-stage startups, although success is not guaranteed. The program is best perceived as an additional enabler for the startups' network, knowledge of the industry, and market validation (Finance no. 3).

Some corporations that operate an incubator program and provide financing will not only screen startups when deciding to invest, but also encourage the startup to seek other sources of finance.

> Our program also focused on linking the company's needs with the innovations being developed by the startups. Once we are sure that they have adequate potential to scale, the CVC [corporate venture capital] will chip in. However, the investment does not come naturally. We also support some of them in getting funding from other investors in our network (Incubator-Accelerator no. 2).

However, financing institutions that did not operate a program or were not linked to one tended to view the programs as ineffective. These financiers pointed to the considerable knowledge gaps in the programs' curricula and support. The programs were perceived as lacking the capability to effectively gauge the business viability of startups.

> Incubation programs are not yet effective for the growth of startups since most of them lack business professionals. The [technology] research aspect heavily influences them, because the programs are mostly run by universities. All the while, the accelerator programs do not provide much help [and] financing institutions can do more once the startups graduate from the incubation program (Finance no. 2).

This impression that the programs might not be effective may be influenced by the fact that Indonesia's most well-known unicorns, Gojek and Tokopedia, were not assisted by such programs. Therefore, it is felt that tech startups can still grow and succeed even without such programs.

Perception of Incubators and Accelerators on Sufficiency and Effectiveness

Of the 10 incubator and accelerator programs interviewed, three suggested that the current number of programs was sufficient. One felt it was insufficient, and the other six did not express an opinion. Three suggested that current programs are beneficial in fostering startup growth while one suggested they were ineffective. Six interviewees did not express an opinion. One interviewee noted the proliferation of university-based programs, but felt that the number is still inadequate.

> Nowadays, the number of incubator and accelerator programs is quite large, especially those from universities, since the Ministry of Education, Culture, Research and Technology requires higher education institutions to have at least one. However, if the question is whether the number is sufficient for startups, the number is still way too low (Incubator-Accelerator no. 9).

Most of the current startups are perceived to be at an early stage of their development, so they lack experience with and basic knowledge of the ecosystem. Interviewees felt that incubators and accelerators are effective when they can provide this knowledge. Such assistance could benefit startups in terms of their financial performance, legal aspects, tech development, and marketing. One interviewee suggested that more programs are needed to provide this knowledge to the many emerging startups.

We need more programs in Indonesia as the number of startups is increasing. Consequently, the number of programs will not be sufficient to assist the startups, especially the early-stage ones in which the founder has just graduated from university. They would require huge assistance from the program to fill the gap between theory and practice in the startup industry (Incubator-Accelerator no. 8).

Overall, program managers felt the number of programs was sufficient and were more concerned about the capacity of both the programs and startups. The effectiveness of a program, they argued, could be measured by two factors: (i) the quality of the program and its ability to assist the tenants, and (ii) the ability of tenants to benefit from the assistance. Startups do not benefit from poor-quality programs, but they also do not benefit from high-quality programs if they cannot absorb and make use of the assistance provided.

Geographic Coverage

There is a disparity in the number of programs operating in each region. The programs are concentrated in Java, especially in the capital city of Jakarta. Therefore, startups located outside of Java may have fewer opportunities to join a program. As one program manager indicated,

> The availability of programs is adequate compared to the number of tech-based startups and SMEs that need to be assisted. [However], most programs are located in Java and Bali. Those located outside these regions are only found in the big cities such as Makassar, Manado, Aceh, Padang, Jambi, Lampung, Pontianak, and Banjarmasin (Incubator-Accelerator no. 4).

The Ministry of Cooperatives and Small Medium Enterprises Regulation No. 24/2015 on Business Incubators requires that there be at least five incubators in each province and at least one incubator in each district or city. However, this target is not met possibly because there are no penalties for places that do not comply. The Indonesian Association of Business Incubators (Asosiasi Inkubator Bisnis Indonesia), a representative body of incubators, also finds that the distribution of incubators is still uneven, with most concentrated in large cities. The manager of an agritech startup in East Indonesia said that while he is satisfied with the facilitation he received from a government incubator in South Sulawesi, he believes that excellent incubators are still concentrated in Java.

Based on an initial mapping, there are 120 programs in Indonesia (Figure 3). However, many programs are no longer running due to the pandemic that started in March 2020. Of the total number of programs, 60% are in Java and are spread across the

Figure 3: Geographic Distribution of Incubators and Accelerators

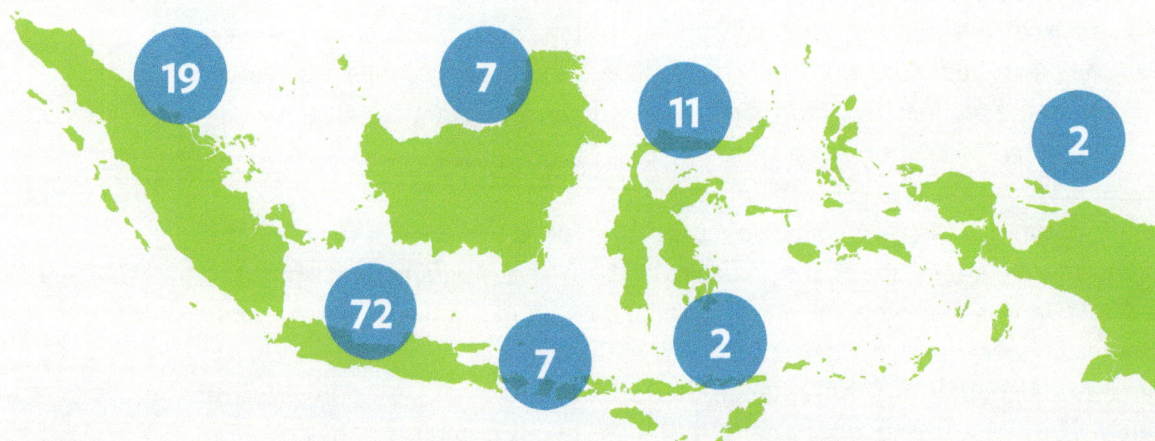

Source: Indonesian Association of Business Incubators. 2020. Daftar Inkubator Bisnis di Indonesia. Jakarta.

two special regions and four provinces—Jakarta and Yogyakarta, as well as Banten, West Java, Central Java, and East Java. Although some of the programs are willing to assist people in other regions, it is difficult and costly for them to do so.

Program Management, Staff, and Mentors

The capacity and expertise of the program's management team is critical to fostering successful startups. The program's staff not only provide advice and guidance to startups, but through their links with other players in the ecosystem, they can also help startups build crucial networks. Furthermore, the program's ability to identify and attract mentors with real business experience is a critical aspect of the incubation experience.

There are a diverse array of incubators and accelerators in Indonesia, and it is difficult to make a general statement about their capacity and the quality of the support they provide. Some are strong and effective, others are less so. The Indonesian Association of Business Incubators acknowledged that some programs are of low quality, with limited management capacity, no or few dedicated full-time staff, few standard operating procedures, a limited network among other players, and limited operating funds. One government official noted that in extreme cases, "local government does not understand the concept of incubators; they think that an incubator is only about providing coworking space" (Government no. 5). Our interviews revealed some of the specific weaknesses of the programs. Often, the nature of the weaknesses was directly related to the type of program sponsorship.

Programs that are managed by a local authority are challenged by the lack of business professionals on their teams, as the management team is often made up of high-ranking civil servants. Furthermore, their program responsibilities are in addition to their other duties as civil servants. Consequently, they cannot fully focus on supporting startups and devote their full energy to them. As one manager noted,

> More often than not, the local government running the incubator program did not consider that the team needed business professionals to fully assist the tenants. The management team consisted of civil servants with other [existing] jobs. Consequently, they cannot focus on nurturing the tenants. The bureaucratic treatment does not fulfill the needs of the startups (Incubator-Accelerator no. 4).

Incubators and accelerators should develop networks for startups and provide access to government agencies, financing institutions, and other businesses in the sector. However, many incubators and accelerators did not have networks, or their networks were limited to a few players.

Meanwhile, there are national government programs that have tried to perform some of the roles of incubators and accelerators, such as mentoring and coaching. Some interviewees said that these efforts are not effective and should be left to incubators and accelerators. Instead, the national government should provide grant funding and enact supportive regulations (Finance no. 4).

University-based incubators are mostly run by experts in research and development (R&D) who have limited business experience. They lack knowledge of startup business strategies, management, marketing, and other aspects. Program managers often do not work full-time on the program because their focus is on teaching and research. Getting them to focus on fostering the tenants can be a challenge.

> They [university incubators] are too fixated on the research aspect of tech assistance and not enough on business assistance. Therefore, they do not fully provide the assistance needed by early-stage startups in facing the real challenge of [operating a] business (Incubator-Accelerator no. 9).

Furthermore, universities may also not be adequately connected to industry.

> If the university incubators involve only their lecturers, then the triple helix approach is not applied.[10] The innovation will not be successful without industry. In fact, industry has to be invited [from the beginning of] the

---

[10] Triple helix refers to university–industry–government interactions in which the university plays the role of incubating technology-based firms (Etzkowitz, De Mello, and Almeida 2005).

teaching process. Only in this way will the students learn what the needs of industry are. They are then able to innovate based on these needs (Government no. 2).

Almost all informants, regardless of sponsorship, noted that the experience level of mentors determines the quality of the incubator. However, most programs lack good mentors and those with sector-specific experience and expertise. One program manager acknowledged that they were unable to provide good mentors to their startup participants.

> The business model [of the program] is quite mature, yet we need more experts—especially those who can help with tech assistance for startups—as mentors. We currently lack that (Incubator-Accelerator no. 3).

Furthermore, it is not easy for an incubator to have the full range of expertise among its mentors.

> In the past, innovation was about manufacturing. Now, it's about IT [information technology]. It is very difficult for incubators to have the range of mentorship available, from manufacturing to IT (Government no. 2).

Many incubators also lack good networks with other players in the sector, making it difficult for startup tenants to develop their network. As the manager of an energy incubator and accelerator noted,

> Our work area is considered specific and complex in Indonesia, since we focus on renewable and clean energy. Therefore, to foster the startups that focus on the same sector, we need partnerships and collaborative programs. However, we currently do not have any, although we have built a network with the Ministry of Energy and Mineral Resources (Incubator-Accelerator no. 6).

Mobility restrictions imposed during the COVID-19 pandemic limited access to incubator and accelerator programs. Programs were forced to replace face-to-face mentoring activities with Zoom meetings. This substitution limited the types of startups that could be mentored, as not all of them had adequate digital access and a stable power supply.

> Although we mainly run digital-based programs, communicating with startups and making sure their needs are met is [was] quite challenging during the pandemic as technical issues increase, such as a weak internet connection during online meetings (Incubator-Accelerator no. 8).

Financing Incubator Programs

A program's main source of financing is based on its sponsorship model, whether by the government, a nonprofit association, a university, or a private business. Programs often combine funds from several sources. In addition to external funds from sponsors, internal funds may be generated from rent paid by tenants and revenue from equity investment. These funds are very flexible because there are no criteria for their use.

Creating a sustainable financing model can be difficult. "It is not easy to establish an incubator," said the founder of an agritech startup (no. 3), "you need a lot of resources." Furthermore, it can take a long time to harvest the returns on the program's investments in startups, and many startups fail, resulting in a loss of investment. Some interviewees noted that while the number of incubators has grown significantly in recent years, it has not grown as fast as the number of startups, which could be due to funding difficulties.

Incubators and accelerators that focus on startups with social impact have difficulty finding private (business) sponsors, as these sponsors want to support startups that can generate profits and a return on investment.

> I believe that the number of incubator and accelerator programs in Indonesia is shrinking over time due to the difficulties in finding independent sponsors with a similar business model [objective] (Finance no. 4).

Incubators that are directly sponsored by the government have a stable source of funding. This provides funds for support, but not for direct investment in startup tenants.

> As part of the government, we receive internal funds from the government institution. However, we cannot invest in tenants because our funding is derived from the state budget. Therefore, our activities consist only of mentoring and providing business matching with investors (Incubator-Accelerator no. 1).

External government financing is provided through startup support programs, notably Tech-Based Pre-Startup Grant Program (CPPBT). Funds are provided to startups in an incubator, and the startup is required to give a portion of the funds (about 25%) to the incubator. When the CPPBT was in operation, it provided Rp200 million–Rp250 million annually to individual startup tenants.

We received external funding from the CPPBT and the PPBT [Tech-Based Startup Grant Program] programs. For the PPBT program, there were no funds that could be used directly by the incubator [for the incubator's operations other than provision of assistance for tenants]. These funds could only be used for startup development. However, we were allowed to keep 20%–30% of the total CPPBT program's funding from each startup (Incubator-Accelerator no. 3).

One incubator noted that the 25% allocation from CPPBT funds was not sufficient.

The grant amount of CPPBT is insufficient to run intensive coaching by incubators as the incubator receives only 25% of the total grant amount for their operational funds. This is especially true for incubators and tenants that are far apart. The ideal grant amount should not be less than Rp250 million (Incubator-Accelerator no. 4).

Furthermore, government grants from the CPPBT were provided based on a plan and budget submitted by the incubator and had to be spent on items specified in the plan. This created problems when support needs changed between the time the plan was drafted and submitted and the time the funds were used. The changes occurred, in part, because the incubator's startups were pivoting.

The CPPBT was terminated in 2020 and the Tech-Based Startup Grant Program (PPBT) was renamed Research-Based Startups (Perusahaan Pemula Berbasis Riset [PPBR]) in 2022. The latter provides each startup with Rp200 million–Rp300 million per year.

University incubators often have stable but limited resources to assist their tenants. They operate within an academic institution, so the programs are regulated under the Ministry of Education, Culture, Research and Technology. It is difficult for the incubator (and its tenants) to raise funds from sources other than university funds because of the ministry's regulations.

In our experience, it is not easy for a university-based incubator to obtain external funding from the private sector. This is because the funds must first go through the institution. Our operations are also highly regulated by the ministerial regulation of the Ministry of Education, Culture, Research and Technology (Incubator-Accelerator no. 3).

Privately sponsored incubators rely on several financing mechanisms, but two types predominate. These are the membership approach and the batch approach. In the membership approach, the corporate partner pays a membership fee to the program to fund its operations. In return, this membership fee allows the corporation to connect with potential startups nurtured by the program.

> Our financial source is mainly our corporate partners. Our partners are generally companies that are used to supporting accelerator programs. They pay a membership fee because we act as the intermediary that brings them together with potential startups. We use those fees to run the program. So far, there are not many obstacles because our corporate partners are very enthusiastic (Incubator-Accelerator no. 8).

In the batch approach, corporate partners provide funds to host a batch of startups in an incubation or accelerator program. The funding is perceived as sustainable (for the incubator or accelerator) because it is typically provided for up to 3 years.

Some corporations may also invest directly in specific startups in the batch, but this investment is only given to startups when they complete the program. A portion of this investment can be used by the startups to pay their fees to the incubator.

> Some startups agreed to pay us in the form of shares at the end of the batch, instead of a monthly fee during the program. Usually we have a [corporate] partnership for 3 years, so it can be considered quite sustainable. We also work together to find potential startups to fund (Incubator-Accelerator no. 7).

Consequently, this mechanism provides startups with pre-seed funding from corporate partners at the end of the batch's program. This funding comes with a provision of another round of funding by the same corporation after the startup exits the program.

2.2   Financing for Startups

Funding is a key support for startups. Most startups begin with a development stage where they create, test, and refine the product. During this time, there is little or no revenue, and therefore startups cannot service credit (i.e., pay interest and principal). Instead, the startup requires a form of funding that does not need to be serviced (i.e., repaid), such as equity, but also grants. Even if the startup begins to scale, revenues may not be sufficient to service the credit for expansion. Here, too, equity is required.

Almost all startups begin with internal or "bootstrapping" funds, which come from the founder's savings or salary from an ongoing job, as well as funds from family or friends. For external funding, there are more than half a dozen potential sources, including angel investors, venture capital, large corporations, equity crowdfunding, banks, incubators and accelerators, grants, and prize money. Angel investors and venture capital are the most prominent. Corporations that invest in startups do so directly or through their venture capital funds (i.e., corporate venture capital).

Until the end of 2020, the government only provided financing in the form of grants through its CPPBT and PPBT programs and prize money in competitions such as the Ministry of Industry's Startup4industry program. In December 2020, the Ministry of Education and Culture launched a matching fund (grants) program called Kedaireka (Box 1).

Box 1: Kedaireka

The Kedaireka program was launched in late 2020 to create synergies in innovation commodification between universities and industry on one platform. A key component is the Matching Fund, which provides grants to improve partnerships between academic institutions, industry, and business. The funds can be used to support innovations produced through university–industry collaborations. The fund was provided Rp250 billion in 2021, rising to Rp1 trillion in 2022.

Under this program, lecturers and/or students from universities and industry parties agree to partner through the Kedaireka platform and design a funding proposal. The funds will be used to

- commercialize technology products and prototypes and advance the growth of the Center for Technology Excellence, Teaching Industry, and Teaching Factory;
- adopt science, technology, and expertise, i.e., through training and coaching, for industry partners;
- execute business plans and business model prototypes for startups created by universities working with business, as well as by students working with alumni and/or business under the guidance of lecturers; and
- establish a Center of Excellence to develop industry partners or solve challenges for industry partners.

Seven other Kedaireka program components were added in late 2022:

- Kedaireka Academy: Digital training platform for university students who receive one-on-one guidance from business professionals
- RekaTalks: A talk show featuring motivational testimonies from Matching Fund beneficiaries
- Match Making Innovation Forum: Quick networking events for university students and/or lecturers with various industries
- RekaPitch: A collaborative program built on business cases selected by industry leaders with access to independent funding
- CEO Mentorship: Intensive sharing sessions led by industry leaders to enhance the exchange of insights and development of students and/or lecturers
- RekaPreneur: Practitioners and academics improve the understanding of pitching, drafting Kedaireka proposals, and business negotiations
- RekaPods: A podcast program in which Matching Fund beneficiaries discuss their innovations and success stories, as well as the benefits they have gained from the Matching Fund program

Sources: Kedaireka; Harususilo, Y. E. 2022. Ditjen Dikti Luncurkan 7 Program Ekosistem Kedaireka. Kompas.com. Jakarta; Hendayana, Y. 2021. Kedaireka dan Matching Fund untuk Akselerasi Reka Cipta Perguruan Tinggi dan DUDI. Directorate General of Higher Education, Ministry of Education and Culture. Jakarta.

Access to finance varies by sector. Popular sectors such as fintech and e-commerce have better access, while the four segments examined in this study—agritech, edtech, healthtech, and greentech—have less access. The latter faces the most constraints. The first three segments are considered Indonesia's rising sectors with increasing investor interest in recent years (Eka 2020). The number of financing institutions for startups is increasing. There may be as many as 200 institutions in total, including foreign institutions. As Indonesia has a large market and community of startups, there is increasing interest from foreign investors.

In terms of best practices for startup financing, many informants referred to methods in Singapore and the Republic of Korea. There, the government provides matching funds (equity) once the startup receives funding from financial institutions or industry.

Angel Investors

Angel investors are high net-worth individuals who invest their own capital in enterprises. They typically step in at the early stages of a startup and provide not only financial support, but also strategic support such as access to networks, mentorship, and expertise that startups need in the beginning of their journey.

Because angel investors in Indonesia tend to remain under the radar, it is difficult to estimate their number and the volume of funding they provide. This also poses a challenge for startups, especially newcomers, as angels are hard to locate and are usually found through personal connections, business networks, or events. One informant mentioned that having personal connections who can vouch for the startup founder helps secure an opportunity to meet with an angel, and that this is more effective than sending cold emails.

In Indonesia, angels can be approached through angel investment networks. They act as a bridge between startups and potential investors and help curate startups for members who are seeking to invest. In Indonesia, there are three angel investment networks that we could identify (Table 4). Over 70 investments were made by the three networks during 2017–2020 (ANGIN 2020).

Table 4: Angel Investment Networks in Indonesia

	Location	Year Established	Members	Description
Angel Investment Network in Indonesia (ANGIN)	Jakarta	2014	100+ (individual and institutional)	Connects members with potential enterprises that apply for funding through ANGIN. Annual membership fee is $300, with add-on post-investment services offered through an advisory business arm
Alternative Investors Group and Advisory (ALTIRA)	Jakarta	2017	15 (individual)	Investor services and capacity development platform for startups and high potential small and medium-sized enterprises
Angel ID	Jakarta	2019	3–5 mentors	Provides pre-seed funding, mentorship, and networking opportunities to tech startups. Also operates A.Incubator in Bandung

Source: Authors.

Venture Capital

Venture capital (VC) is a common source of funding for startups. VC firms provide funding at various stages, although a startup typically needs to have a minimum viable product, traction in the market, and some level of maturity. VC is a hoped-for source after a product or service has been introduced to the market and capital is needed to scale up. VC firms or funds also provide access to business networks, industry figures, and other funding opportunities. Young startups may opt to enter a venture builder—a company that develops numerous startups and eventually becomes the parent company with the largest share.

Domestic VC funds have traditionally supported SMEs and continue to do so. Local VC funds borrow from banks to invest in enterprises that are usually already established and thus less risky. This limits the role of the VC fund in acting like venture capitalists for startups and taking risks. In some cases, local VC firms simply channel money from banks and act like banks because they charge interest even though they also engage in profit sharing (Haliding 2018; Sinamo 2019).[11] Hana (2017) says that because a local VC firm relies on banks, it has difficulty financing startups because startups have no revenue to service credit from a VC firm, but the VC firm must service its loans from the bank.[12]

Understanding this shortcoming, the Financial Services Authority (OJK) Regulation No. 35/2015 provides a framework for local VC firms to receive funds from domestic and foreign investors, aside from banks. The VC firm can still retain a link with a custodian bank to improve investor confidence. The Financial Services Authority believes that this source of funds would enable local VC firms to provide equity to startups (Gunawan 2020). However, it remains uncertain whether many local VC firms have the ability and courage to set up a venture fund.

Other recent regulatory changes are also likely to boost VC investment in startups. Ministry of Finance Regulation No. 48/2018 allows VC firms with equity investment in SME firms—with sales of up to Rp50 billion—to be exempt from dividend tax. This is an increase from the previous threshold of Rp5 billion in sales.[13] Local or foreign VC firms registered with the Financial Services Authority are eligible for this tax treatment. The tax treatment does not apply to dividends of a publicly listed firm (investee) and is granted for a maximum of 10 years.

---

[11] The profit-sharing activity is recognized by the Financial Services Authority (Investor.id 2015).

[12] Hana (2017) is quoting the Association of Indonesia's Venture Capital and Startups on this point.

[13] However, Amvesindo said that the regulation has not addressed the industry's needs, namely a 25% reduction in capital gains tax (Aldila 2019).

More recently, some improvements have been made under Law No. 11/2020 on Job Creation. Government Regulation No. 34/2021 on Foreign Workers Utilization exempts startups from the need to obtain approval from the Ministry of Manpower if they wish to recruit foreign talent. There is also the newly established Presidential Regulation No. 10/2021 on Investment Business Activities and its revision in Presidential Regulation No. 49/2021, which allows startups to receive foreign investments below Rp10 billion, unlike other types of businesses that can only receive investments above that amount. The investment must be located in a special economic zone.

One obstacle for VC firms is the difficulty of exiting an equity investment. OJK Regulation No. 35/2015 (Article 16) provides three exit options: (i) initial public offering (IPO), (ii) private placement, and (iii) buyback. An IPO can be complicated and costly (Lenggogeni and Subiakto 2020).[14] The other two strategies are better, but not without challenges, as it is not always easy to find buyers at a reasonable price. Moreover, in these two strategies, capital gains are taxed at 25%, which is high compared to Singapore where there is no capital gains tax. Exiting through an IPO results in a capital gains tax of only 0.1% (Ika 2017; Article 4 Law No. 17/2000 on Income Tax).[15] Therefore, exit mechanisms can be improved to encourage more investment in startups by domestic funders.[16] Exit issues may also explain why some Indonesian startups are obtaining financing in Singapore, where exiting is easier and less costly (Table 5).

The VC scene has grown considerably in recent years. It includes stand-alone venture capital firms and funds, corporate venture capital, and growth funds (joint funds). In 2020, there were 65 venture capital firms registered with the OJK. These include local VC firms as well as a few local-foreign joint ventures. Additionally, there are many foreign VC firms and agents operating in Indonesia that are not registered with OJK. An informant from a financing institution stated that, based on their data, there are a total of about 200 financing firms and agents investing in Indonesia.

> This is still an evolving stage where the interest of local companies must be encouraged to fund the startups. Venture capital is the most suitable scheme for financing startups, but the regulations in our country are different from those in other countries. Venture capital practices have yet to be developed in Indonesia. Meanwhile, many venture companies have emerged in the form of LLCs [limited liability companies] and cooperatives, which is good (Government no. 5).

---

[14] Singapore also allows for easy and less costly IPOs (Assegaf 2020).

[15] Some scholars insist that IPO is not an exit strategy. It is a way to mobilize funds from the public (Firdaus 2021).

[16] Aside from equity participation, Article 2 of OJK Regulation No. 35/2015 stipulated that VC can finance startups through (i) quasi-equity participation, (ii) financing through the purchase of bonds, and (iii) financing of productive business.

Table 5: Foreign Incorporation in Indonesia and Singapore

Indicators	Indonesia	Singapore
Ease of Doing Business 2019 ranking	73	2
• Starting a business	140	4
• Protecting minority investors	37	3
• Enforcing contracts	139	1
Registration	Foreign investment company takes up to 1.5 months to provide the documentation	Company registration is relatively simple; can be done online within 24 hours
Requirement for foreign ownership	Foreign investment should be minimum Rp10 billion (excluding land and building); foreign ownership could only be 100% in industries outside the Negative Investment List	Companies can be 100% foreign owned with minimum paid-up capital of S$1.
Directors and shareholders	Directors can be foreigners, but the director of personnel must be Indonesian. There must be a minimum of 2 shareholders.	Minimum 1 resident director (can be nominee director for compliance) and 1 shareholder
Tax	Corporate income tax: 1%–22% depending on industry and level of profit VAT: 11% Capital gains tax: 25% for company, 30% for individual	Corporate income tax among the lowest in the world: 0%–17%. VAT: 7% Capital gains tax: 0%
Venture capital firms	Incentives for VCs investing in startups: 0% tax on dividend on sales Rp50 billion	Many VCs are based in Singapore or will only invest in companies with a Singapore entity. Government provides incentives for entrepreneurs and VCs. Many overseas investors pour money into Singaporean VCs to support startups
Corruption Perception Index by Transparency International 2021 (scale to 100)	85	38

VAT = value-added tax, VC = venture capital.
Sources: World Bank. 2020. Doing Business 2020: Comparing Business Regulation in 190 Economies. Economy Profile Indonesia. Washington, DC; World Bank. 2020. Doing Business 2020: Comparing Business Regulation in 190 Economies. Economy Profile Singapore. Washington, DC; Iras.Gov.Sg. 2022. Inland Revenue Authority of Singapore; BKPM. 2017. Penanaman Modal Asing di Indonesia. Jakarta; Paul Hype Page & Co. 2022. How to Register a Company in Indonesia?; Cekindo Editorial Team. 2022. Capital Gains Tax Indonesia: A Guide to Accounting and Tax Reporting. Jakarta.

In 2019, a total of $582 million was invested in Indonesian enterprises by VC firms, a considerable increase from $325 million the previous year. The number of transactions at each stage of enterprise development also increased between 2017 and 2019, with seed funding accounting for the largest number of transactions (Figure 4).

The money provided by the VC fund is one benefit, but market validation is another.

> If one just wants to get working capital, they can turn to banks. Going to venture capitalists like us could be beneficial because startups get market validation from us. They can also get a higher valuation and more growth in the future (Finance no. 3).

Figure 4: Funding Transactions by Stage

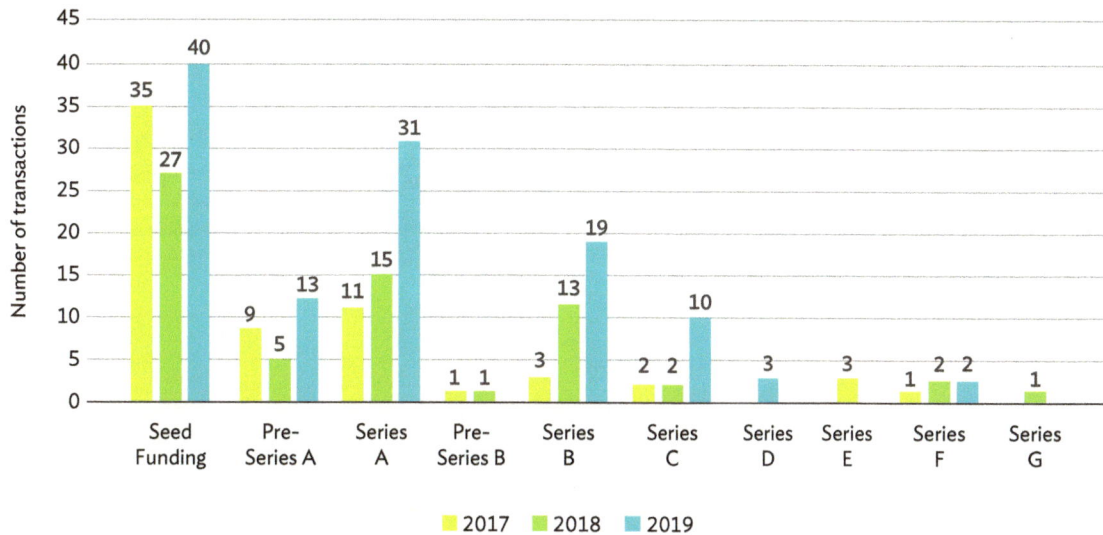

Source: Eka, R. 2020. Startup Report 2019: Scaling Through Technology Democratization. *DailySocial*.

Despite the high number of seed funding transactions, there is still a lack of adequate funding for startups at the earliest stage given the high demand. However, not all startups are yet ready to obtain funding from investors.

> I was observing the pitching session where, in my opinion, the ideal situation is collaboration between startup and investors. But to my surprise, almost all [startups] are reluctant to give their equity to the investor. They would rather pay the interest rate to the investor. Probably, the startups [feel] that decision-making becomes more complicated when investors are part of the management. It could also be that they are afraid that their idea will leak out (Government no. 5).

An important development in the Indonesian startup scene is the rise of corporate venture capital (CVC) (Table 6). CVC can be provided in several ways, such as from a corporation's VC fund, directly from the corporation, or through incubators and accelerators, as noted earlier. CVC typically pursues a synergy agenda to foster startups in line with the corporation's sector activities and company vision. Therefore, CVC not only provides funding to startups, but also offers immediate access to a client-buyer (the corporation) or to broader markets. Publicly available data indicate that CVC has not yet invested in cleantech, but some have invested in edtech, healthtech, and agritech.

Table 6: Corporate Venture Capital Firms or Funds in Indonesia

Firm or Fund	Parent Company
Central Capital Ventura	BCA
Sinar Mas Digital Ventures	Sinar Mas Group
MDI Ventures	Telkom Group (state-owned)
Telkomsel Mitra Inovasi	Telkomsel (state-owned)
Mandiri Capital Indonesia	Bank Mandiri (state-owned)
BRI Ventures	Bank BRI (state-owned)
Lippo Digital Ventures	Lippo Group
Astra Ventura	Astra Group

Source: Authors.

A growth fund is a joint funding initiative that brings together several VC firms. Such funds target above-average growth startups at later stages of development. In 2020, at least eight growth funds were in operation (Eka 2020). Two notable examples are Centauri Fund, which was launched by MDI and KB Financial Group and provides pre-Series A to Series B funding, and EV Growth, which was launched by East Ventures, Sinar Mas Digital Ventures, and Yahoo! Japan Capital.

Equity Crowdfunding

Two of the three OJK-licensed equity crowdfunding (ECF) platforms, Bizhare and Santara, offer fundraising for SMEs. However, ECF platforms are still a nascent investment channel, and their usage by startups is unknown and likely to be small. ECF platforms have formed the Indonesian Association of Equity Crowdfunding Platforms (Asosiasi Layanan Urun Dana Indonesia). An informant from a financing institution mentioned that such platforms should be bolstered as they could serve as an additional source of funding for startups, especially those in the early stages. There seems to be a tendency to use crowdfunding for traditional small businesses, with expansion to tech startups coming later. The informant noted,

> Other instruments such as crowdfunding are quite effective; starting from this year, the tone of equity crowdfunding in Indonesia has become crowdfunding for companies, such as minimarkets and restaurants. In the future, maybe something like this can be applied to digital startups, because investors want quick returns, while investing in startups takes time. Soon our startups will have more variety in funding sources (Finance no. 4).

Bank Credit

Banks are still reluctant to lend to startups because they are deemed risky, especially early-stage startups. Loans need to be serviced, and startups have little or no revenue in the early stages. Startups also cannot provide the required documents such as a balance sheet or a profit and loss statement. However, the manager of one incubator said that some of their startups benefited from the relaxation of bank lending practices during the COVID-19 pandemic. This suggests that some startups may obtain bank loans as a means of financing.

Generally, however, startups are not interested in obtaining bank loans. And banks, in their opinion, are not interested in funding startups whose revenues are not yet stable and who do not have collateral.

> Funding through banks is impossible. They set the interest rate too high and require collateral. Figuratively speaking, even after selling all my belongings including clothes, I would not be able to repay the loan. We [startups] are just starting the business. I would rather look for investors or sell the products to the local government (Agritech no. 8).

Funding from Incubators and Accelerators

Some incubator and accelerator programs provide funding, mainly in the form of grants. The terms vary; some offer funding as part of the program participation package, while others select startups after they reach a certain stage of the program or upon graduation. A few incubators and accelerators provide equity funding. Regardless of whether incubators and accelerators provide funding, participation in a program can increase a startup's exposure to the financing ecosystem through the program's networks and events such as pitching competitions that investors attend.

Matching Financing Supply and Demand

While there are a number of potential financing sources, a key question is whether the supply adequately meets the demand of startups. This is a difficult question to answer. Not every startup that wants finance is worthy of receiving it. Many may not have a viable product or a quality team that can make the venture a success. It is well recognized that a high proportion of new enterprises, including startups, fail within the first few years. Investing in startups therefore always involves risk, and it is the role of financiers to assess the risk and provide finance for those startups that have a good chance of success. It may be that financiers are conservative in their assessment of risk and therefore appear to not be providing the supply that meets the demand. However, it may also be that there is sufficient potential supply of finance, but insufficient investment-worthy projects from startups, even if the risk is not assessed conservatively. In other words, the quality of demand may be weak.

Given these factors, the players interviewed for this report did not provide a clear answer to the question of whether volume of supply is adequate and whether there is a sufficient number of quality startup projects being proposed on the demand side. One informant said that both the supply of and demand for finance are sufficient, but the real challenge for startups is being able to compete for funding by demonstrating their startup potential.

> Regarding supply and demand, I can say [that it is] sufficient, because there are also many foreign funding institutions looking for startups. On the other hand, there are actually many startups in Indonesia, and [the number] continues to grow. The challenge is how to compete for funds in the market (Finance no. 3).

Another informant felt that there are not enough angel investors and that the supply is insufficient, but only for startups that are not, in fact, ready for investment. Another informant felt that a number of factors influence the supply and demand for finance and that some startups have not approached financiers.

> Regarding supply and demand for startup funding, I can't say generally because it depends on product readiness, relationships with other investors, and passion of venture capital. There are several startups that have approached some venture capital [firms] who want a deal, but some [startups] haven't (Finance no. 2).

Several informants mentioned a lack of funding for startups in the early stages, which could come from angel investors. However, one informant from an angel network mentioned that the capital is there, but the challenge is in matching supply and demand. The network's experience shows that in addition to the startup's potential, an angel investor's willingness and readiness to invest in a startup in a specific sector also determines successful matching. Earlier generations of investors or more traditional angel investors are less familiar with some of the newer sectors.

> We saw that from the demand side there were a lot of new startups, but it didn't seem like they had met the supply side. On the supply side, there is capital, but it might just not match, maybe the startups that are looking to raise funds are not on the investors' radar (Finance no. 1).

Competition for funding from angel investors is high. An angel network team member we interviewed mentioned that only 4% of startups that submit proposals to the network get showcased, and only 1% eventually receive an investment. This may reflect the quality of startups applying, but also the profiles of current member investors. There may be a mismatch between the interests of investors and the types (sectors) of startups submitting proposals.

The criteria vary between investors, by sector, and by stage of development of the startup—although there are some clear commonalities. The criteria mentioned—and used—by financing institutions are listed in Table 7. The quality of the startup's founder (or founders) is unanimously cited as a key criterion, and almost all informants indicated that startups struggle to meet this criterion. This is especially important for early-stage startups, as there is no product to assess yet, only the people. Some informants also mentioned the team as a criterion that startups have difficulty meeting, which can be seen as an extension of the founder's character. Investors see the founder's capability as an indication of whether the startup will survive and grow. "In our opinion, the most important and arguably the biggest cause of failure is the founder," said one financier (Finance no. 4).

Table 7: Investment (Financing) Criteria

Aspect	Investment Criteria Mentioned by Financiers	Do Most Startups Struggle to Meet the Criterion?
Personnel	Founder's background and quality	Yes, especially early-stage startups
	Team condition	Yes, especially early-stage startups
Business	Business model	Yes
	Scoped market potential and opportunity	Yes
	Product-market fit	Yes, especially startups looking to scale
	Ability to compete in the market	Not mentioned
	Traction and number of customers	Yes, especially startups looking to scale
	Revenue generated	Not mentioned
	Social impact	Not mentioned
Other aspects	Network (e.g., prior engagement with the financing institution)	Not mentioned

Source: Authors.

Meanwhile, for late-stage startups, the degree of product-market fit (product validity) and market traction that a startup has achieved are considered important criteria that startups struggle to meet. As one financier noted,

> Startups that are most likely to receive our funds are those that already have traction or revenue in the market. In the VC world, they're called 'early-stage in pre-series A or series A.' But we don't rule out the possibility [of funding] startups at an earlier stage, if they have aspects that are strong for us to validate, such as the background of the founders, or if they are already working with us (Finance no. 3).

On the demand side, ecosystem informants noted that not all startups want equity funding, at least not in the early stages. They may fear the due diligence required by an investor. Startups may take out a loan for initial working capital instead of equity, because they want to avoid the complications associated with having other people involved (e.g., investor shareholders). Startups worry that their ideas may be changed or stolen if external shareholders are added.

How much and what kind of funding a startup needs also depends on their business model and desired growth trajectory. Such aspects need to be given consideration when determining the best financing schemes and instruments for startups at different stages of development, in different sectors, and with different business models.

> Indeed, not all startups need funding. But we often hear that the success indicator of technology startups is how much funding they have been able to raise, while arguably important indicators such as surviving in the market [and] positive market ratings would be more representative. Not all startups want to get equity investment because the commitment is very large (Finance no. 1).

One informant added that startups prefer loans from industry partners because the process of obtaining a loan from a bank is more complicated (Government no. 5).

In addition, a majority of Indonesia's commercial activity and funding sources are concentrated in Jakarta and the Java-Bali area. As a result, sources of capital, including angel investors, are unequally distributed across the country. While it may be more difficult for institutional investors to expand into these regions, angel investors may be encouraged to fund the growing number of startups in these areas. One informant, who works for a VC firm that is a subsidiary of a state-owned enterprise (SoE), has sought to broaden outreach by using the SoE's branch offices across the country. The VC firm tailors its programs to specific regions through startup centers in the company's branches.

> Big startups come from big cities (Jakarta, Bandung, and Yogya), and other areas still lack them. We have a special program for regions; there is a startup center in our SoE's branch offices, and every year we have a program for coaching and scouting talent from the regions (Finance no. 4).

Furthermore, some regulations still constrain investment, including from foreign investors. Several informants mentioned tax regulations and the business environment (i.e., ease of doing business). As a result, some startups are asked to establish a holding company in Singapore through which Singaporean and other foreign investors can channel their investments.

Finance for Agritech, Edtech, Healthtech, and Cleantech

The number of funding transactions for agritech, edtech, healthtech, and greentech is still far below other sectors, but there has been robust growth in all sectors except greentech. Fintech, Software-as-a-Service (SaaS), and e-commerce continue to attract the most funding (Figures 5, 6, and 7).

Healthtech is performing well and gaining access to funding. Halodoc, which raised $65 million in 2019, and Alodokter are successful startups that have grown into large companies and may be creating a growing interest in these sectors. Newman's and TeleCTG received undisclosed amounts of seed funding in 2017 and 2020, respectively. Several Indonesian VC firms, such as East Ventures and Intudo, are active in funding healthtech startups.

In greentech, there are few funding transactions for startups. Of the four financial institutions interviewed, only one has invested in a greentech startup. Investors in Indonesia may not be comfortable investing in greentech startups (and some in agritech) whose business models are capital-heavy and based on deep tech. This could be due to financial interests (i.e., investors want a quick return) or sector interests (i.e., investors lack sector knowledge), which can limit the value an investor can bring to a startup. As one financier noted,

> There are no cleantech startups that have received investment yet. We have showcased them several times, but it was not successful. Maybe there are not so many investors who are familiar with the sector (Finance no. 1).

The agritech sector has received about $33 million in funding from seed to Series B stage since 2013, though the actual number is likely higher because the amounts raised are not disclosed in all cases (Putera and Tang 2020). Tanihub is an example of a successful agritech startup.

In edtech, Ruangguru received $150 million in funding in 2019, and Zenius is another successful startup. A World Bank (2020a) survey found that Indonesian edtech firms acquire capital from a variety of sources, with the most common sources being angel investors and VC. More than half of the firms surveyed acquired funding from more than one source.

Figure 5: Startup Funding Trend Based on the Business Vertical, 2017–2020

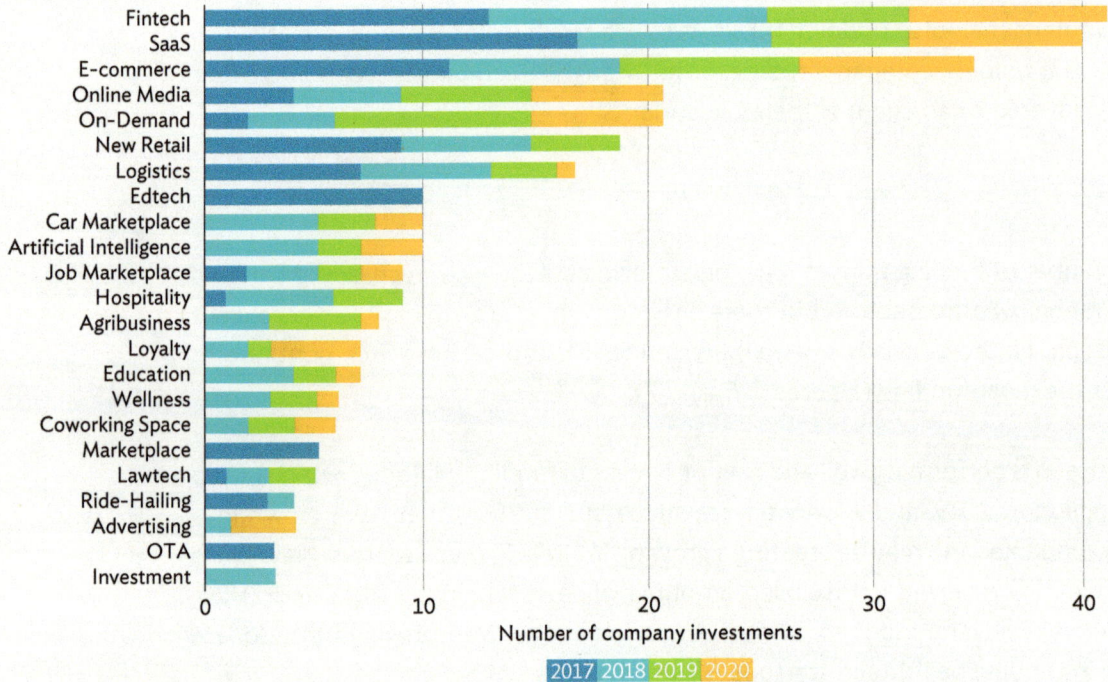

OTA = online travel agency, SaaS = Software-as-a-Service.
Source: Eka, R. 2020. Startup Report 2019: Scaling Through Technology Democratization. *DailySocial*.

Figure 6: Startup Funding Trend Based on the Business Vertical, 2021

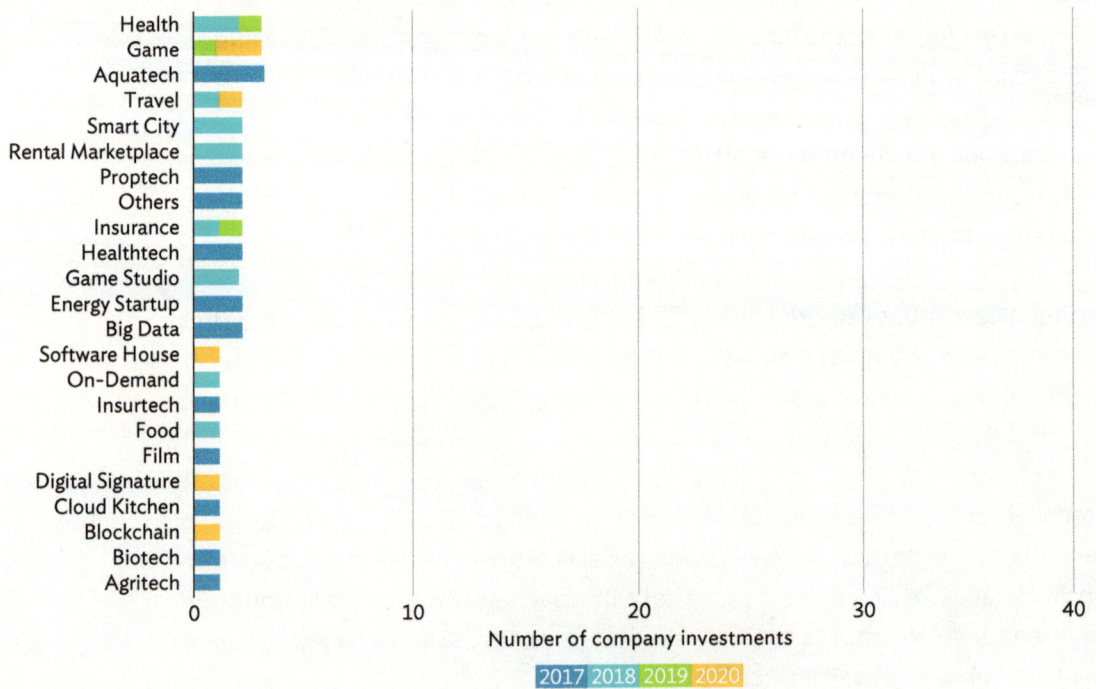

Source: Eka, R. 2020. Startup Report 2019: Scaling Through Technology Democratization. *DailySocial*.

Figure 7: Startup Funding Trend Based on the Business Vertical, First Quarter of 2022
(million)

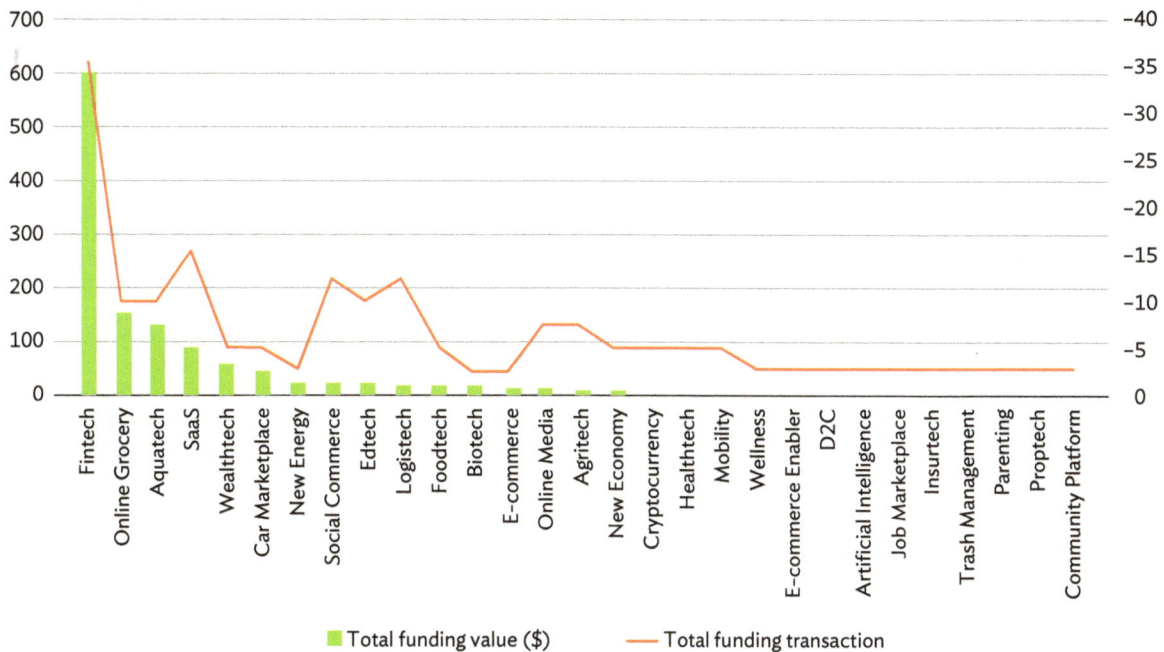

SaaS = Software-as-a-Service.
Source: Eka, R. 2020. Startup Report 2019: Scaling Through Technology Democratization. *DailySocial*.

2.3 Government Programs and Policies

Government programs conducted by various ministries in the last 5 years have generally been supportive. These programs raised awareness, encouraged participation, and nurtured youth enthusiasm for entrepreneurship. They have been good for promotional purposes. Among the programs, incubators appreciated the CPPBT and PPBT programs (Box 2) of the Ministry of Research and Technology (Kemenristek) and the National Research and Innovation Agency (Badan Riset dan Inovasi Nasional [BRIN]). According to informants, these programs have been successful in motivating incubators, universities, and local governments to support startups. Other ministers have also offered programs. The Ministry of Communication and Information Technology (Kemenkominfo) provides the Gerakan Nasional 1000 Startup Digital program, the Next Indonesia Unicorns (NextICorn) program, and the Startup Studio Indonesia program. The Ministry of Industry provides the Startup4industry program. The Appendix lists and provides details of many government startup programs.[17]

---

[17] An ADB brief argues that government and other support is best provided at the city level to build local ecosystems (Bachtiar, Sawiji, and Vandenberg 2022). The brief was written by the same authors as this report.

Box 2: Narrow or Broad Approach to Selecting Startups for Support

In 2015, the national government launched two related programs, one for pre-startups (Tech-Based Pre-Startup Grant Program [CPPBT]) and the other for startups (Tech-Based Startup Grant Program). Applications were received from across the country, and the most promising 200 ventures were accepted. These startups were given funding and were required to enroll in an incubator. A portion of the funds given to the startups for CPPBT, about 25%, was passed on to the incubator. These two programs were important in spurring the startup-incubation process. However, some difficulties were also encountered.

First, during 2015–2019, the graduation rate of startups from the CPPBT to the Tech-Based Startup Grant Program was only 11%, which seems low. Indeed, developing a good prototype during the CPPBT program did not necessarily lead to the creation of a viable startup. Second, these programs focused on incubators and did not include accelerators, nor did they form networks with venture capital and other investors. Third, they may have targeted too many startups, resulting in the inclusion of some (or many) unviable ones.

The last point is particularly difficult for program planners. Accepting many applicants can be seen as positive, as it promotes economic inclusion and can potentially have a broad impact. However, as noted earlier, nonviable startups may be included. On the other hand, a narrower, more competitive approach would accept fewer applicants, but only those of high quality. This approach is more akin to that used by venture capitalists when deciding to invest.

In 2020, the two programs were rebranded and subsumed into a new program, Startup Innovation Indonesia. Efforts were made to address earlier concerns, notably, accommodating and linking with more actors from the ecosystem.

Source: Authors' interview with Government no. 2 respondent.

However, informants underlined the importance of program sustainability. The CPPBT and PPBT programs, for example, were dormant in 2020 after budget reallocations due to COVID-19. One incubator manager said that government programs should embrace a functional approach rather than an event approach. This means that the focus should be on following up with actions after events. Another incubator manager said that government programs are scattered and that they would have a stronger impact on startups if they were consolidated.

There are other issues with government programs. Informants said the administrative aspects can be burdensome. Startups that receive support have to submit many reports for accountability purposes, which often seem unnecessary. Another incubator manager said that while the CPPBT and PPBT are basically good programs, they are too rigid in their implementation. Sometimes the targets are set too high for the startups to achieve in a short period of time. The other downside of CPPBT and PPBT funding is that the incubators are required to spend the entire operating budget during the year. They cannot save funds for later use. As a result, incubators cannot accumulate savings for the future.

In terms of policies and regulations, startups usually have difficulty registering new products because product categories do not exist in the national standards certification system. Some informants mentioned that it is not easy to do business in Indonesia. Others expressed concerns about the tax rate, which is lower in Singapore. As a result, many prefer to register in Singapore. In addition, many informants have high expectations for the enactment of Law No. 11/2020 on Job Creation, which they said would boost business (e.g., relaxed restrictions on hiring foreign talent, lower paid-up capital requirements for startups in special economic zones, reduced restrictions on foreign investment in the education sector).

The need for regulatory sandboxes was voiced by startups in three of the four sectors. This approach was introduced to the fintech industry in the United Kingdom in 2016 (Chen 2020). The objectives of a regulatory sandbox are to support innovation, raise competition, and achieve financial inclusion. Testing the product in a regulatory sandbox allows both the firm and the regulator to learn: the regulator learns more about the innovation and how to regulate it, while the young firm can innovate without being burdened by excessive regulations. Referring to the experience of fintech firms, the startups we interviewed suggested that the same mechanism could be applied to agritech, edtech, and healthtech.[18]

In Indonesia, the regulatory sandbox for fintech was introduced in 2017. Under the supervision of the central bank, a firm could test its innovative e-money and e-wallet services in a live environment.[19] Meanwhile, in 2018, the OJK started a regulatory sandbox for crowdfunding and peer-to-peer lending.[20] After 12 months or less, the regulator will consider whether to grant the firm a business license (Batunanggar 2019).

Burhan (2021) explains that the Ministry of Information and Communication Technology will assess the application of the regulatory sandbox in industries aside from fintech, and priority could be given to healthtech. Healthtech, where innovations can carry high risks for consumers, may be best suited for a regulatory sandbox. Researchers at the Center for Tropical Doctors at the University of Gajah Mada are exploring the opportunities and challenges of a regulatory sandbox in support of malaria eradication (Adelayanti 2020).

Outside Indonesia, the Ministry of Health in Singapore has created a regulatory sandbox for telemedicine in 2020. In agritech, supporters of regulatory sandbox in other sectors explain how innovation could boost agriculture. Leow (2020) reports that the Ministry of Trade and Industry and agencies such as the Singapore Food Agency and Enterprise Singapore will set up a regulatory sandbox for agri-food farms. There are also possibilities for applying the regulatory sandbox to edtech. Simpson (2020) lays out a step-by-step approach for setting up a regulatory sandbox for edtech.

---

[18] None of the informants from cleantech mentioned the importance of the regulatory sandbox.
[19] Central Bank Regulation No. 19/2017 on Implementation of Financial Technology.
[20] OJK Regulation No. 13/2018 on Digital Innovation in Financial Services Sector.

At the global level, some scholars are doubtful about the benefit of the regulatory sandbox. Appaya and Haji (2020) said that it is too early to draw conclusions because the framework has only been applied for 4 years. The benefits depend heavily on the way it is designed, implemented, and monitored. Accordingly, a study of fintech firms that have had experience with a regulatory sandbox in the United Kingdom found that the benefits can be significant, but most startups do not anticipate the burden involved (Deloitte 2018). While adjusting to the sandbox, they must still run their business.

2.4   The Founders, the Team, and the Talent

Whether a startup survives or fails depends largely on the quality of its founders. The most important characteristics of a founder include vision, passion, perseverance, and entrepreneurial spirit. While ecosystem factors external to the startup are important, the critical role of founders was emphasized repeatedly in our interviews. Furthermore, the founders assemble and are part of a core team responsible for technology, product design, management, marketing, and other factors. The quality of the team and the ability of team members to work together under the leadership of the founders are critical to the survival, sustainability, and success of the venture.

An official from the Ministry of Communication and Information Technology quoted Gojek's founder as saying, "Anyone can steal your idea, but no one can steal your execution" (Government no. 3). Thus, the execution of a good idea is important, and informants unanimously agree on the importance of the founders and the team in this regard.

One important aspect of the quality of founders is experience.

> Incubator and accelerator programs surely have a role in assisting the growth of the startup industry. However, they are not as influential as the quality of the startup founders themselves. Nowadays, startups are being built by those who are familiar with the industry, and some may have previously worked for a unicorn (Finance no. 4).

A financier noted the experience gained from working in other successful startups.

> On the issue of the low success rate of university incubators, that's because the tenants are fresh graduates who do not understand how to run a business. I would suggest that they gain experience first. Nowadays, the founders of newly developed startups are former employees of a unicorn. This is good because they start developing a startup when they have already become accustomed to the culture and environment of the industry (Finance no. 4).

Another informant referred to a study that said most successful founders are around 40 years old and thus have gained experience in their earlier years. Investors can quickly tell if a founder has experience, and this will be a key consideration when assessing a funding request.

> The founders who have no experience but dare to jump into meeting the investor are indeed running the risk of losing the opportunity (Incubator-Accelerator no. 9).

Founders need to have a clear vision and not just follow the trend of "simply doing daily business as usual" (Incubator-Accelerator no. 7). With a vision of what they want to achieve, founders create a team. The team may initially consist of only the founders, and then expands to bring in personnel to drive key areas of the business. Creating and maintaining a solid team is as important to investors as the product.

> The first criterion to invest is to see the founder and the team. We need to ensure that they have positive character [traits], such as the ability to work together, respect each other, [and are] committed. We can think about the product together if we have a team with these qualities (Finance no. 2).

The team must have a shared vision, with mutual trust and commitment needed to ensure team unity and cohesion. When the vision is not shared, internal conflict usually results. An initially solid team can fall apart as well when money problems arise, including how profits are shared. To maintain cohesiveness and trust, the business must be managed transparently. There are many examples where a startup fails because the team breaks apart.

> I once witnessed a case where a [startup with a] very good product—only a few steps to thriving—failed when the team disputed with each other. What a pity! (Government no. 4).

> The team could be very enthusiastic in the beginning, but some months later started to break up. Because of this, we started to recruit a psychologist this year who will help us understand team cohesiveness when we select tenants (Incubator-Accelerator no. 1).

Team members should bring different skills and expertise to the startup. A dream team is one with skills that complement each other.

> For us the team profile is important. A good startup should at least consist of a hacker, a hipster, and a hustler (Incubator-Accelerator no. 2).[21]

---

[21]   A hipster provides innovation, a hacker supplies technological expertise, and a hustler is in charge of marketing and market development.

A team that consists only of innovation and technology experts is prone to fail. It may be excellent at inventing, but if the product does not sell, all the effort will have been in vain.

> It is not desirable to have a team with a good product but not be able to sell it. A combination of product and marketing is sufficient (Finance no. 3).

Another informant believed that management skills are also essential. Startups will certainly fail if they are not able to allocate money accordingly and manage their cash flow. Financial management is crucial, particularly when the founders are usually tech experts who are unable to manage an organization. Once a startup runs out of cash, friction arises. Many informants pointed out the importance of a business and entrepreneurial mindset, which is lacking in many startups.

The team provides the initial talent for the startup, but as the enterprise expands, more talent is hired to work with the core team. Finding enough talent, whether as part of the core team or as part of the startup's larger workforce, is both important and challenging. There may not be enough talent, in part due to competition for talent from other enterprises, including unicorns and large traditional businesses. The "talent deficit" was frequently cited by informants.

> Those who desire to develop startups and create platforms are faced with the reality that we simply don't have talent. We have a limited number of engineers. The idea is there, but it cannot be materialized if we don't have engineers. Therefore, the government is very keen to launch a digital talent scholarship (Government no. 3).

> The main problem is talent. One study has shown that by 2030, the shortage of talent will hinder people from developing startups because it will be very expensive to get talent. On the other hand, the graduates of vocational high schools who remain unemployed are those who come from information and communication technology [programs]. Apparently, what they learned was [from] obsolete programs. Their teachers are not updating their knowledge, while technology is changing very fast (Incubator-Accelerator no. 9).

Foreign investors are interested in Indonesia—because of its large market and the growing community of startups—but they are careful in assessing whether startups have access to the talent needed to succeed.

2.5 Product and Timing

For a startup to thrive, it must develop a product-market fit. This means that the product solves a problem, addresses a need, or satisfies a desire so that customers are willing to buy it. Informants highlighted the importance of the product and its market fit to the success of a startup. There are four aspects to this.

First, the idea or problem must be validated. Most startups fail when the product idea lacks originality or when it only slightly modifies an existing product without adding much value. These startups simply "follow the trend" and fail to see new problems that need to be solved or that there is a new demand that is unmet. They may be inspired by the success of unicorns like Gojek and Tokopedia, but fail to recognize that they need an original idea. As one government official noted,

> I told the startup founders to look around and think clearly. We have so many problems that require solutions, why only focus on on-demand transportation and e-commerce? (Government no. 4).

Even at the problem evaluation stage, it is good to have businesspeople on board who can think about the problem the product will solve.

> The difference between academics and businessmen: the first start from the solution, the latter start from the problem (Incubator-Accelerator no. 9).

Incubators can play a role in problem validation when screening new startups. Once the problem is validated, the startups can join and have a greater chance of success with the subsequent validation of the product and business model.

> Starting in 2010, we apply new tools for validation in the selection process. The tools will help us identify the aspects of problem validation, product validation, and business validation. With these, we were able to increase the graduation rate of our tenants (Incubator-Accelerator no. 1).

Second, there is market validation. It is possible that the idea is brilliant, but there has to be market demand for it. The entrepreneur needs to ask: would it fit or meet consumer needs, and is there a large potential market? At this stage, innovators need to ensure that the product really does solve a real problem for other businesses or people.

Third is business model fit. Not only should the product be suitable for the problem and the market, it should also be produced and delivered through the right business model. The business model ensures that customers like the way the product is offered. Again, incubators play an important role in creating this fit, which is in fact a large part of what an incubator offers.

Fourth and finally, there is competitiveness. The startup should know and understand its competitors in the market, offer a unique solution, and market the product at a price point that both attracts buyers and generates a profit for the startup.

An aspect closely related to product-market fit is timing. An idea may be innovative, and the product may normally be in demand, but it may not be the right time to enter the market. Conversely, a startup may also be successful because it launches a product at the right time. For example, a bad timing situation might be an economic downturn, inflation that reduces purchasing power, a recent flood of similar products, or a lack of consumer knowledge. A product may not be successful because it is ahead of its time. But it may also be that a product may be launched just when a new demand arises; it might be "right on time" and successful in riding a wave of consumer interest.

Timing is rarely mentioned as a factor in startup success, but according to one informant, it can be very important. The COVID-19 pandemic provides a good example of timing in both a positive and negative sense. Some startups struggled because demand for their products and services declined due to the lockdowns. In contrast, demand for other products and services increased (e.g., home delivery, telemedicine, and web conferencing apps). How the pandemic affected startups is discussed in more detail in the analysis of the four market segments later in the report.

Support Needed at Each Stage of the Life Cycle

3

Startups progress through a series of stages in which success at a lower stage is necessary to advance to a higher stage. These stages present different challenges, often referred to as structural barriers, which may relate to product development, finance, human resources, or other elements (Wymer and Regan 2005; Spender et al. 2017). Just as challenges differ by stage, the support required to overcome them will also differ or the importance of a particular type of support may differ. There are different ways to categorize the development stages of startups (Box 3). Our analysis uses three stages: (i) formation, (ii) growth, and (iii) scaling (Box 3).

The formation stage includes problem identification and solution validation, in which the idea is turned into a product or service and tested. The basic business model is also formulated. The growth stage involves producing, marketing and selling the product, and making adjustments based on customer feedback. The business

Box 3: Number of Stages in a Startup's Life Cycle

Over the course of their life, startups go through a number of stages. However, there is no consensus on how many stages there are or how each is defined. Incubators may have a different idea of stages than financiers, who link development stages to funding.

Alpha JWC Ventures (2022) sees seven stages of funding, ranging from the pre-seed stage, which includes research, to the initial public offering stage when shares are sold. Meanwhile, Indeed Editorial Team (2021) suggests eight stages adding a "bridging loan" stage prior to the initial public offering.

Most incubators and accelerators consider fewer stages. The GAIN (2022) suggests five stages: (i) conducting research; (ii) building a minimum viable product or MVP; (iii) gaining traction; (iv) improving the final product; and (v) accelerating. Meanwhile, Startup Commons considers only three stages.[a] The first is the formation stage, where the product idea is developed; the team is created; and the vision, mission, and strategies are laid out. The questions of what (i.e., the product), for whom (i.e., the customers), and why (i.e., the problem-solution) are answered. The second stage is the validation stage of committing and validating. In this stage, the MVP is finalized, while continuous iteration is conducted, and a pivot made if necessary. The third stage is the growth stage where the venture is well established and scaling occurs. In this stage, the venture focuses on growing the user base (i.e., customers), raising funding, and adding new talent to the core team and the enterprise.

[a] Startup Commons. Starting Point for Ecosystem Development.
Source: Authors and references cited.

model is modified and solidified. The scaling stage is about expanding the business, increasing output, and growing the customer base.

We interviewed 18 supporting actors in the ecosystem, including managers and staff from incubators and accelerators, government agencies, and finance institutions. They were asked to indicate the key area of support needed in each of the three stages. The areas of support chosen were business assistance, legal assistance, technology assistance, market assistance, and funding. Figure 8 provides the results and shows an interesting pattern: in the formation stage, business and technology assistance are most important, while in the scaling stage, marketing assistance and financing are most significant. The middle (growth) stage requires a more even distribution of the five support factors.

Figure 8: Support Needed at Different Stages of the Life Cycle

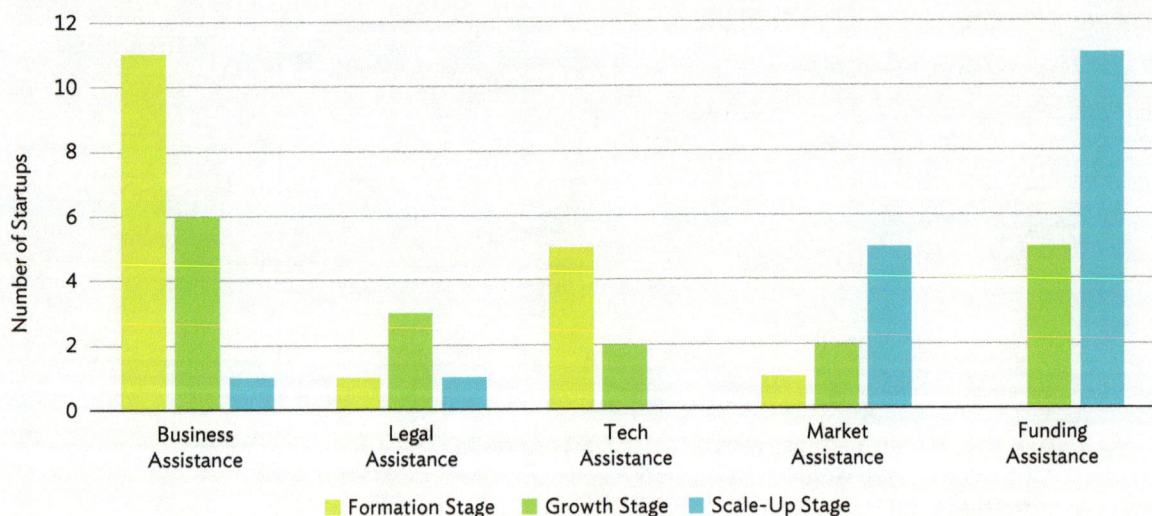

Source: Authors.

Formation Stage

The formation stage focuses on product and business development. In this stage, most support actors feel that business (management) assistance is most important, followed by technology support. Most startups encounter problems with their product and business direction at this stage—they cannot optimize the technology and have difficulty commercializing it, often because founders lack business experience. As one government official noted,

This stage mostly relates to how well the startup knows the technology or how it can commercialize the product. There are a lot of startups that only copy other ideas without having a business mission of their own (Government no. 5).

Therefore, startups need support in building the business foundation. In doing so, team formation and team management need mentoring. At this stage, the core team needs to know how to optimize the advantages of combining members with different types of education and experience.

Another support is technology assistance and advice on product-market fit. Some startups have difficulty developing their idea into a product, while others have trouble refining the product's technology.

Most startups still struggle to transform their ideas into a product. Their product usually has a 'technology readiness level' below 5. We have to support them through incubation by developing their idea into a good product (Incubator-Accelerator no. 5).

In the formation stage, startups also need legal and marketing assistance. Legal support includes help with company registration, regulatory compliance, and intellectual property registration.

In the formation stage of the startups, they need support for innovation empowerment in the ecosystem. We have to support them in finalizing their products and help them with certification of products and other legal aspects (Incubator-Accelerator no. 1).

Growth Stage

The growth stage focuses on proving market fit by selling the product. In this stage, some changes in startup support are required. Business assistance is still the most important type of support, but funding emerges as an important concern, according to our informants. In this stage, startups also need to develop the product, improve management, and find business partners and investors.

Startups have to validate their product in the mass market and need a partner to help them. They also [often] lack a developed business model, and the ecosystem needs to facilitate some support, such as product validation, product support, and specific business strategy guidance (Government no. 4).

The ecosystem can assist startups with these issues, including helping them manage a growing team. Internally, startups need to regularize their staff and improve human resources management. Furthermore, startups in the growth stage need additional funds to further improve the product and ramp up production. Legal assistance is needed for brand registration and protection, drafting contracts with their suppliers, and complying with tax regulations. In our interviews, startups said they need legal assistance to deal with government regulations.

> As for regulation, the ease of doing business for startups needs to be optimized; the regulation in Indonesia is still too complicated, especially for startups with foreign investors (Finance no. 1).

At this stage, marketing assistance and tech assistance are still important.

Scaling Stage

The scaling stage is about expanding the business. The startup already has traction in the market and needs more funding and assistance to grow its market share. We have found that startups that want to enter this stage have difficulty accessing funds. They may need support to approach multiple sources for funding, and this means expanding their network to meet suitable investors.

> In the scaling stage, startups must have an advanced action plan and will need funds to run it; therefore, startups need support to relate to the investors (Incubator–Accelerator no. 2).

Market assistance is also needed to improve collaboration and networking with other businesses, notably suppliers. Legal and business assistance in this stage would include continuing the product licensing and certification process started in the stability stage. Meanwhile, business assistance includes mentoring the team on expansion, financial management, and human resources management.

Agriculture and Agritech

4

Agritech startups benefit from access to incubators and accelerators, mentors, funding, and government programs, like startups in other sectors do. But the agriculture sector also has unique elements that require dedicated support. Access to demonstration plots is one, and the low digital literacy of potential customers (farmers) is another. Indeed, developing the user base is particularly challenging because the intended clientele consists of farmers who lack funds to purchase tech products and services, do not understand new technologies, and are averse to adopting them.

Incubators and Accelerators

Almost all of the agricultural startups interviewed reported receiving support from incubators, especially those based at universities. Six of the 10 startups we interviewed had founders who were friends on campus. Two of these six startups were formed while the founders were still students at the university. For them, building a startup on campus was beneficial. The campus environment is conducive: they have plenty of opportunity to learn, collaborate—and compete—with friends. Only a few startups gained entry to private-sector accelerator programs.

Agritech startups benefit from the same type of support as other startups. This includes access to coworking space, training and coaching, as well as networking. Some incubators also assisted startups in preparing for pitching events and participating in exhibitions. Incubators also help startups address legal issues, such as business registration and permits and securing intellectual property rights.

In general, the roles played by incubators and accelerators fall into three categories, according to informants. First, these programs should provide startups with professional mentors. These mentors can develop talent and assist the startups in business management, marketing, personnel and administration, and paying taxes. One informant suggested that mentors should help with both software technology and business development. Mentors do not necessarily have to be employees of the incubator.

> An accelerator like Village Capital could be used as a model for [providing] mentorship. It opens up the possibility of [accessing] external mentors who are experts in the field. They [mentors] are not necessarily the staff of Village Capital but are ones that perfectly suit the needs of startups (Agritech no. 7).

It is important that startups are trained and coached by individuals with sector expertise. Incubators should also consider the specific needs of a startup and its development stage when assigning mentors.

> Good incubators are those that tailor their mentoring and coaching to the needs of the startups. It is recommended not to mix startups at different stages (Agritech no. 9).

Second, incubators and accelerators open startups' access to investors, customers, and players. Thus, it is important that incubators have a wide network to connect startups with financiers, large companies, and government agencies. Agritech startups need to network with local government agencies to facilitate them in testing their product in demonstration plots. An informant also suggested that incubators and accelerators are, in fact, curators who provide important information to convince investors.

> What startups really need are market access and financial access. It is urgent for incubators [and] accelerators to provide this access (Agritech no. 4).

Third, the incubator or accelerator should provide a community for startups. Sometimes startups can meet with their peer groups in seminars or workshops held by the incubator or accelerator. Startups listen and share problems that encourage the founder and the team. Through this community, startups gain a wider network of contacts. Most often, the community develops as an informal group, like a WhatsApp group. Startups of the same vertical (sector) can learn from each other much better than if they are mixed with startups of different verticals.

Access to Finance

Not surprisingly, most informants said that financing is very important to the success of startups. Some noted that it is more important than enrollment in an incubator, with finance considered the key factor, whereas incubators are facilitators. Financing, whether through equity from angel investors, VC, or even grants, is vital, particularly in the formation and stability phases when important activities such as research, market analysis, and testing are being conducted.

Some startups said that the ideal funding scheme is one that starts with grants in the early stages. Grants help the startup build a prototype, test the product, and conduct market research, which are costly and are done before revenue is generated. Grants can take the form of a research grant or a competition reward.[22] One startup interviewed had received a research grant from a state-owned corporation, while five others received grants from the private sector.

Banks are not considered an important source of financing.

> The bank would not understand the business model of a startup, which is different from that of small and medium enterprises. Banks also apply terms that are not beneficial to startups (Agritech No. 9).

Equity investment should be sought when the founders have some confidence in their product and business model and can therefore negotiate more effectively with investors.

> Effective funding starts with a grant. If investors enter while ideas are still raw, they will dominate and founders will be less motivated to strive in the later stage (Agritech no. 7).

Early-stage equity funding is often supplied by angel investors, but their number is small in Indonesia. Two of the informants were funded by a venture builder. They felt they were lucky because few investors are willing to invest in startups that have not yet achieved market traction.

Obtaining equity funding depends on several factors. First, investors must have confidence in the founder and the team (not just the product and business model). Second, the pitch should be to investors who are familiar with agritech, the agriculture sector, and startups. Investors who are not familiar consider startups too risky. An informant said that many investors are still very careful when it comes to investing in this area, and that more success stories are needed.

> It takes examples where an agritech startup has grown to the level of a unicorn in order to gain the confidence of financing institutions. Unfortunately, this is still lacking in Indonesia. Hence, investors still doubt the profitability of agritech (Agritech no. 9).

---

[22] In 2018, the Ministry of Industry started organizing yearly competitions with rewards.

Third, securing the initial investment is crucial, as investors are more likely to invest in a startup if it has already received an investment. Fourth, a founder must use the right language when making the pitch. A startup founder revealed that sometimes founders use only general terms and forget to use the specific terminology that investors expect and that would demonstrate the founder's deeper understanding. This is particularly true for startups from outside Jakarta.

Several informants noted that more venture capital would be available if there was a better investment climate, particularly for foreign venture capital. Some informants noted that regulations and taxation of foreign investment in startups are far greater than in Singapore. As a result, VC funds often want Indonesian startups to register in Singapore.

> They [venture capital] are more comfortable and secure with the regulations in Singapore. There, the law is on their side; they can exit the startup funding when they need a capital gain. This is why one cannot find Indonesian unicorns registered locally. Foreign investors do not dare to enter the country. This has become commonly agreed that if you need an investor, you need to have an entity in Singapore (Agritech no. 7).[23]

Government Programs

Almost all informants are familiar with government programs. Six of 10 startups interviewed have received grants from the Ministry of Education, Culture, Research and Technology.[24] Three other startups have been invited to events sponsored by ministries such as the Ministry of Information and Communication Technology and the Ministry of Youth and Sports. In general, startups appreciate government initiatives that support them. The grants from CPPBT and PPBT are considered very helpful for startups in their early stages, particularly because the amount is significant.

> There are many programs from other ministries. However, they are not as complete as PPBT, where a startup can receive hundreds of millions of rupiahs. The mentors are also professionals from the private sector (Agritech no. 2).

However, the CPPBT and PPBT programs may not be sufficient for agritech startups as they are only for 1 year. Startups can take up to 5 years to reach a sizable customer base, said one informant. Some aspects of CPPBT and PPBT reporting requirements can be burdensome as well. Purchasing hardware is preferred over market research, in part because the former is easier to verify. However, for startups, the latter may be needed more.

---

[23] This applies mainly for Series A funding and above. There are foreign investors that provide pre-seed and seed funding for startups that are registered only in Indonesia.

[24] The Ministry of Research and Technology handled the grants but the ministry was abolished in April 2021, and the program was absorbed by the Ministry of Education, Culture, Research and Technology.

Programs in the agriculture sector that educate farmers about startups can be useful. For example, it can take considerable time, energy, and money for startups to introduce their products and services at the farm level. If the government had a specific program in which startups could introduce their products, they could reach many farmers at once instead of visiting them individually.

One program mentioned by an informant is the Farmers' Corporation of the Ministry of Agriculture.[25] This program was initiated by President Joko Widodo to adopt best practices from Malaysia and Spain to improve the welfare of farmers and fishermen. The term "corporation" comes from the partnership between farmers and state-owned, locally owned, or private corporations that purchase farm produce. A farmers' corporation can take the form of a cooperative or similar legal entity. If it can attract a large number of farmers to join, startups can provide new technologies and innovations to farmers at low cost.

Bachtiar et al. (2020) stated that the share of agricultural workers using the internet is only 2%, while the sector accounts for 27% of total employment. Policies and regulations that improve digital infrastructure in rural areas would help increase demand for startup products and services that use the internet. Startup services offered over the internet also require electricity to charge smartphones and other devices.

The government can also provide digital literacy training for rural communities. Bachtiar et al. (2020) pointed out that the inclusion of agriculture in the digital economy—and thus the use of startups' goods and services—is hampered by low digital literacy. Farmers are risk-averse about technology owing to low levels of education and are unfamiliar with new products offered by startups. Consumers need to be educated, and this could take the form of promotional events or exhibitions where startups can present their products.

> Startups like us could do consumer education, but our power is limited. Government has the power to do it massively. Other actors such as the community and NGOs could also help (Agritech no. 9).

The government is an important actor in the development of the talent pool. It can adapt the curriculum in vocational schools to produce the talent needed to staff agritech startups. Startups can only succeed if they have access to skilled talent.

There is also a government program for small-scale credit (Kredit Usaha Rakyat [KUR]) provided through banks and targeting farmers and small and medium-sized

---

[25] Ministry of Agriculture Regulation No. 18/RC 040/4/2018 regarding Guidelines in Farm Area Development Based on Farmers' Corporation.

enterprises (SMEs). All state-owned banks are given a target for disbursement of KUR. KUR can be used to purchase agritech products and services. However, one informant said that banks have traditionally been more interested in approving credit for motorcycles than credit for investment in farm equipment.

As food self-sufficiency has become part of the government's vision, agritech startups that can help achieve food security are given priority by state-owned corporations, including their corporate venture capital funds. These do not necessarily have to be agriculture-specific state-owned corporations; they could also be state-owned banks. This was reported by an agritech manager and confirmed by an informant from a venture capital fund.

> In the agriculture sector, the government sets up a collaboration mechanism in which BUMNs [Badan Hukum Milik Negara, state-owned corporations] and their affiliates finance and provide logistics support to agritech (Finance no. 4).

At the local level, the governor of West Java has initiated the Digital Village program (Program Desa Digital) and the Millennial Farmers program (Program Petani Milenial). Under these programs, villages are provided digital infrastructure, digital literacy training for farmers and others to join the online marketplace, and training on how to use the Internet of Things to boost farm productivity. Program Petani Milenial encourages young people to become farmers by giving agriculture a positive image, such as using digital technologies in farm management. These programs have been beneficial to some startups in West Java and could be beneficial for startups in other provinces. Other innovations from startups seeking to innovate financing and from the Farmers' Cooperation are also being tested (Box 4).

Local governments are also important, as startups often need access to demonstration plots (and ponds) and need to conduct market research for product validation. These activities could be enhanced through collaboration with local government agricultural extension workers.

> We need facilities to do research. For agritech in fisheries, our products should be held in the ponds. If local government could open our access to various ponds, that would help us a lot (Agritech no. 10).

Box 4: Encouraging Farmers to Adopt Technology

A startup founder explained how startups can make their services affordable for farmers. "In the beginning, we sold our product to farmers. However, after some time, we learned that it was best to rent it out instead of selling it. We invited farmers to use the product and pay for the service [rent it] on a monthly basis. As renting is much cheaper than buying, farmers are willing to adopt the affordable technology."

In addition, he said that in order to push the use of the technology, startups would need to prepare a scheme that allows payment for their service after the harvest. For example, chili farmers will pay after 6 months, potato farmers after 3 to 4 months, and so on. This scheme is only possible if startups and farmers partner with banks.

He mentioned that the policy of the Farmers' Corporation would be beneficial for both startups and farmers using technologies. "If the government can organize a large number of farmers under the Farmers' Corporation, startups can negotiate with the corporation instead of just individual farmers. In this concept, the corporation is professionally managed. It [suggests] what to plant and when based on market data and weather forecasts. In the meantime, farmers can focus on cultivation: they produce a certain quality and quantity, using innovative products from startups."

Source: Authors' interview with Agritech no. 1.

Government Regulations and Tariffs

The procedures for obtaining permits and licenses for businesses have improved, as they can now be done online in a relatively short time, and the procedures are clear. Incubators will often help startups. However, agritech startups felt that the biggest hurdle was in obtaining intellectual property rights, particularly patents. Some informants complained about the slow process of patent acquisition.

> At the scaling phase, we have to ensure that our product is not illegally copied by other parties. However, it takes us a long time, up to 4 years, to acquire [a patent] (Agritech no. 1).

Certification to the Indonesian National Standard is also difficult to obtain for startups that produce hardware. Regulations for drones are even more complex. In addition to certification as a small flying object, startups must obtain a flying permit to conduct tests and demonstration. The regulation on flying permits is currently being drafted by the Ministry of Transportation and the National Air Force.

Regulations to promote the use of environmentally friendly products in agriculture do not yet exist in Indonesia. Unlike neighboring countries, Indonesia does not have regulations to reduce the use of pesticides. One informant said that this is why he started exporting his product to Malaysia, Thailand, and Viet Nam, where governments require farmers to reduce the use of pesticides. If such a regulation existed in Indonesia, the market for pesticide reductant—a liquid mixture that helps farmers reduce pesticide use—would be more promising. This non-pesticide substance is mixed with 50% of the usual amount of pesticide without affecting the quality of the result.

> The absence of regulation on pesticide reduction gives more homework to startups like us. We have to educate the market, to give farmers information, sometimes personally. With regulations to comply with, our problem is reduced to providing solutions (Agritech no. 7).

Startups that produce hardware also expressed difficulty in paying high import tariffs on parts that are not made domestically.

> Machines and batteries for drones are still imported from [the People's Republic of] China. If we have to pay a high price for imported goods, then we would also put a higher price for our drone; then we cannot compete with [the People's Republic of] China's [drones] (Agritech no. 2).

High prices for some imported parts can also have a negative effect on startups' research in Indonesia. One informant gives the example of Malaysia, where imported components for research activities, such as machines for prototyping, are tax-free.

Talent Development

Like other sectors, the availability of talent for startups is an important factor in the success of startups. Talent is developed in various ways, most notably through the education system, internship programs, and mentoring. One agritech startup noted the need for a good education system, but also the benefits of internships.

> Education quality in Indonesia has to be made uniform so that graduates are ready to work or at least [can] be trained quickly. We need quality talent to be competitive. The program of the Minister of Education and Culture—so called Kampus Merdeka Program—fits our needs. The program requires university students to do internships outside of campus for 6 months. Startups could be the place for this internship (Agritech no. 9).

At university, the talent pool is best developed using the triple helix approach (university, private sector, and government), according to an informant. This means inviting experienced professionals to campus to teach and mentor startups developed at the university. It is no longer relevant for the campus to keep the old approach in which lecturers teach business but never do business. Quality mentors—experienced professionals—can also nurture talent in startups that are enrolled in non-university incubators and accelerators.

Nature of the Market (Aging Farmers, Trust in New Technology)

Agriculture is characterized by aging farmers. Many do not have smartphones, cannot afford an internet connection, and have limited digital skills. Older farmers are also risk averse when it comes to new investments. One informant said that farmers generally have the mindset of relying on government transfers and subsidies (Box 5). With this mindset, they do not understand why they should pay for technology. Many do not understand what a contract between parties means. After signing a contract, they are not aware of their obligations.

Educating customers, particularly providing information to farmers, was mentioned frequently by informants. There is low trust in new brands (Greenhouse Team 2021). Consumer education is particularly important in the context of the digital divide facing the agriculture sector and aging farmers.

> It takes a lot of effort to educate and introduce new products to society. If we only rely on our promotion activity it would be difficult to get people's attention. It takes support from the government. When government [officials] talk, people will listen (Agritech no. 3).

Thus, government, including local governments, can play an important role in facilitating consumer education (Box 5). Programs such as Digital Village and Millennial Farmers would give the agriculture sector the opportunity to get accustomed to digital technology. At the same time, this helps startups better understand the agriculture sector so that the business model designed meets farmers' needs.

Box 5: Strategy to Address the Aging Farm Sector

A tech startup founder gives his observations on aging farmers.

"The average farmer in Indonesia is above 50 years old and technology is not their cup of tea anymore. Startups like us should, therefore, smartly target millennials, instead. We need to encourage them to farm by attaching technology to gain their interest. Sometimes, we are asked to join socialization meetings in which high officials are present. Before the visit, we always require two things from the village head. First, they have to ensure that the invited farmers bring with them their young family members, be it a child, a nephew, or even a grandchild. Second, the village youth group should join the meeting. Then in the meeting, we say to the young invitees that if they are willing to become farmers, we will teach them how to fly drones. Flying drones is challenging for youth. If they can master the techniques, they can get a certificate."

"When we introduced our startup activity, at first, many people were skeptical about farmers being able to use a smartphone to operate their farms. Not all farmers had a smartphone. Yet, we are sure that in every household at least one phone could be connected to the internet, particularly with school-from-home during the pandemic. Thus, with the help of a young family member, the farmers can install the application and bring the smartphone to the field. The young family member could help inform the farmer on the time to spread fertilizer, give water, etc."

Note: The two paragraphs are direct quotations.
Source: Authors' interview with Agritech no. 1.

The COVID-19 Pandemic: Disruptions and Opportunities

Although agriculture is one of the sectors that continued to grow during the pandemic (Ryza 2020), most agritech startups were very much affected, mainly because demand for their products or services dropped significantly. However, some took advantage of new opportunities or downtime to improve a product or modify the business model. In general, most informants were happy and relieved to survive the pandemic.

The pandemic had different impacts depending on the type of customer.

> The impact of the pandemic could differ between startups with a B2B and a B2C model. Most of our customers are corporates whose cash flow has been disturbed because their traders delayed payment (Agritech no. 7).

In some cases, the pandemic forced startups to revisit their business model and change customer focus to reduce risk and ensure adequate demand. One startup relied heavily on business-to-business (B2B) sales in the past, but then focused more on business-to-consumer (B2C). Being agile and able to pivot was one of the lessons learned from the pandemic.

Startups also noted delays in interacting with other players in the ecosystem. The following were mentioned: delays in executing approved projects with the government and private sector; delays in marketing and other exhibitions; and delays in receiving CPPBT and PPBT grants in 2020 due to budget reallocation. Lockdowns also affected imports and exports, and field research activities could not be conducted.

However, startups also described some advantages. One startup founder made good use of slack time during the pandemic to find an international online competition, the MIT Solve Sustainable Food System Challenge 2020, in which she entered and won. Many introduced coping mechanisms to streamline their startups by reducing salaries and refocusing resources on quick gains. Other startups used work-from-home time to improve their products. For example, one founder said he was able to focus on completing a web application and bringing it to market. The application provides same-day delivery of produce from the nearest farmers to consumers. Another new product—a drone for food delivery—was developed to cope with reduced personal mobility. Indeed, the pandemic has created new opportunities and needs for the use of technology.

> The pandemic has taught us an important lesson: the private sector and government officials became more aware that the use of technology is extremely urgent. They are now contacting us for further collaboration (Agritech no. 4).

For some, demand increased rapidly due to lockdowns.

> Our user numbers grew very quickly in the last 6 months due to internet penetration and the pandemic. Now we have 10,000 farmers [as clients] all over Indonesia, mostly urban farmers in Jakarta, Medan, Surabaya, and other cities in West Java, Sumatera, and Sulawesi (Agritech no. 9).

Challenges at Each Life Cycle Phase

The needs at each life cycle phase of agritech startups are similar to those of startups in other sectors, but with some variations. The main issues are access to farmers and plots to test new products and developing the market among farmers, many of whom are poor and adverse to or unable to adopt new technologies. The challenges and the support needed at each stage of the life cycle are shown in Table 8.

Table 8: Challenges and Support Needed During the Life Cycle

Aspects of Challenges		Challenges in Each Phase			Support Needed
		Formation	Stability	Scaling	
Startup	Product	Research and product testing	Business model development, product validation	Supply chain and distribution channel, patent acquisition	Research grant by government; corporate social responsibility; seed investment by angel investor; access to demo plot, fishponds; regulation on product patent; regulation on imported parts; regulatory sandbox for agritech
	Fund	Grants, awards	Grants, equity investment	Equity investment	Access to investors and big companies; regulation on foreign investment
	Get to know customers	Reaching customers	Convincing customers	Securing loyalty	Consumer education and collaboration with local government, quicker implementation of Farmers' Corporation
	Founder/team capacity		Cash flow, marketing, hiring	Finance, competition for talents with unicorn	Quality mentorship, talent pool development
Agriculture	Aging farmers	Digital divide	Risk averse	Dropping out of contract	Consumer education, including digital literacy; adoption of Millennial Farmers program
	Fund for investment		Farmers do not have money to buy the product		Collaboration with banking, industry; credit for small farmers
	Infrastructure	Internet, electricity	Internet, electricity, roads		Adoption of Digital Village program
	Entry barriers		Monopoly by established players		Collaboration with local government, closer supervision of fair competition by local government

Source: Authors.

In the formation stage, conducting research is the main activity. It is difficult for most startups to obtain research funding, and research is often self-financed. According to an informant, the formation stage is like "hell on earth" for startups because they spend money but do not generate revenue. Singapore was mentioned by an informant as innovation-friendly because any prospective research there is funded by the government. Indonesia could adopt this approach.[26] Sometimes funds can be obtained from the corporate social responsibility funding of large companies or seed investment from angel investors.

In the stability phase, the product is validated in the market and the business model is refined to find the best way to deliver the product to customers. Developing the business model is easier when consumers know the importance of the technology and are willing to invest in it. In agritech, such consumer education can be carried out with the help of agriculture extension workers. This collaboration is valuable not only because it reduces the startups' effort to educate customers, but also because it can help select early adopters (farmers), which can provide a demonstration effect that attracts other customers. Local governments can also play a role in promoting the benefits of agritech.

> Startups like us have limited budget to demonstrate the impact of technology to farmers in order to raise the adoption rates. It would be helpful if startups are endorsed by local government in a program like Millennial Farmers to show farmers some success stories. We can also collaborate with the local government to organize demonstration plots where we can test our business model and validate the market (Agritech no. 4).

Another startup also highlighted the importance of the demonstration effect.

> We conducted research in 2019 and found that farmers have problems [to solve] but are unwilling to adopt the solution offered. Farmers are usually resistant to new technology. Since they are farming out of necessity and simply to survive, they cannot afford to take a risk that will affect their livelihoods. The only chance is to demonstrate that our solution can improve their productivity. We only need five farmers in the village to test the result. If it works, the story will spread automatically to the whole village (Agritech no. 5).

The business model must take into account the potential market. Many potential customers are poor farmers who do not have the funds to invest in innovation. The government can play a role in supporting demand. For example, a drone-maker

---

[26] To a certain extent, in the CPPBT and PPBT programs, the government is financing the prospective research activities through the incubators.

hoped farmers could buy the drone with funds from the KUR credit scheme. However, the price of the drone is above the ceiling for KUR loans, which is Rp100 million. A higher loan ceiling would help the startup sell more drones.

In the scaling phase, four key issues arise: intellectual property, talent, financing, and supply chain and distribution. Startups often need to register the patent for their product to prevent others from copying it. Some informants complained about the slow patent registration process, as noted earlier in this report. Startups also require more talent to fill out their team. The question is whether talent with the needed qualifications is available and not attracted by other firms.

> We need more talent, and this is the most important issue as we grow. However, we are competing with unicorns who can pay talent with much higher salaries (Agritech no. 10).

To achieve scale, startups need additional finance. While grants, prize money, and small-scale equity investments are available in the early stages, larger equity investments are needed to achieve scale. These can be secured through foreign venture capital.

> Startups might not face difficulties in finding financing institutions locally in the early stage. However, it is even more difficult to find local financing institutions for follow-on investments. Follow-on investments are more suitable for foreign investment because they require a lot of funds and a longer period of investment (Agritech no. 7).

Finally, as the customer base expands, the startup needs to manage the supply chain and distribution channels. Some informants noted that they are blocked by existing enterprises, which is a barrier for newcomers to enter the market and scale up. This is evident in the fisheries sector, where existing players monopolize the market and dictate the price, according to one informant. They hamper the development of efficient distribution channels, particularly the direct connection from producers to consumers.

> Players in [the] fisheries sector are like water in a pond: calm but dangerous. They work exclusively in groups. Those outside these groups surely do not get any profit (Agritech no. 10).

This exclusivity makes it difficult for startups to enter the fishery sector and provide new methods that can reduce transaction costs and improve the distribution chain using digital technology. Competition between old and new players is far from balanced. Hence, governments should be vigilant to ensure fair competition.

Education and Edtech

5

The education sector has undergone significant change over the last 20 years. Edtech can support further change now and in the years ahead. The onset of the Reformation Era in the early 2000s marked the transfer of responsibilities from the central to the local level, including education. Later, between 1999 and 2020, the Constitution was amended to mandate education as a development priority with one-fifth of the budget to be spent on education. Compulsory education of 9 years was introduced in 2003. Consequently, children's access to primary and secondary education increased. Unfortunately, the increase in spending has not contributed significantly to better learning outcomes (Rosser and Fahmi 2016). For example, the country still lags behind its neighbors in scores on international standardized tests such as the Programme for International Student Assessment.

The quality of education could be improved through the use of information and communication technology (World Bank 2020a). Indeed, the application of digital technology has the potential to significantly improve teaching and learning. Indonesia, like other countries in the region, suffers from a "learning crisis" due to the low quality of education. Edtech may not be able to solve the crisis on its own, but it can be an important part of the solution. There are three main types of solutions: (i) independent online learning at home; (ii) remote learning connected to the school, college, or university; and (iii) in-school learning. Artificial intelligence can assess a student's level and provide them with level-appropriate lessons, addressing the problem of students falling behind in the classroom. Also, teachers can use edtech to monitor learning progress by tracking the results of exercises, quizzes, and tests in real time. Using this information, they can modify their teaching to meet the needs of the whole class and individual students.

The COVID-19 pandemic gave edtech a major push due to the shift to remote learning. Much of this development is based on existing applications that enable remote learning (Zoom, Google Classroom), but there have been innovations as well. The pandemic opened eyes and changed perceptions of the possibilities of digital solutions, which will likely have a lasting impact on education. However, challenges remain (Table 9).

Table 9: Perception of Schemes and How to Improve

Actors	Difficulties	How to Improve
Incubators and accelerators	Startups in different stages of development are granted similar support. Incubators and accelerators are still disproportionately spread out and concentrated in Java and Bali.	• Support should be adapted to the development stage of the startup. Incubators and accelerators should help solve business problems in the early stages. In later stages, startups need help networking for funding. • Better coverage can be provided outside of Java and Bali.
Financing institutions	The majority of investors focus on e-commerce to make high profits in a short time. Few investors are interested in education.	• Impact investors could pay more attention to edtech, which can have a big social impact. • For startups to thrive, they need funds and business development assistance.
Government programs	Government programs create the momentum edtech startups need to enter the market. However, the programs depend on constantly changing budget allocations.	• The government needs to come up with a mechanism to provide continuous support to early-stage startups.

Source: Authors.

Incubators and Accelerators

The edtech startups interviewed had mixed experiences regarding incubators and accelerators. Some joined, some did not want to join, and a few had difficulty getting accepted.

> There are still few incubators compared with startups. Unfortunately, these few incubators are not really providing mentorship. Instead, they only act as event organizers (Edtech no. 5).

> We haven't gotten access to an incubator program, but we are still trying to. The incubators mostly focus on nurturing startups with clear prospects. We are a social startup; our values are different from theirs (Edtech no. 6).

Meanwhile, those who make it into an accelerator program can receive high-quality mentoring.

> I participated in an international accelerator [Google Accelerator]. It was different. The program was very well organized; the team was all out in all processes. They guided us on how to optimize resources. We had a demo day at the end and many investors were invited. They all came because they knew they would get something valuable. It might be different when a local incubator or accelerator is inviting investors. They might not be as enthusiastic for that (Edtech no. 2).

Financing Institutions

For investors, the education sector is still not considered as attractive as e-commerce. Most of the informants agreed that this is the main reason why funding for the education sector is limited.

> In e-commerce, customers can buy [a startup's] products every day. In education, students only register twice a year, in March and September. This differentiates education and e-commerce, which investors need to understand. It is not possible to expect the growth rate in this sector to be the same as in e-commerce (Edtech no. 1).

One startup interviewed was fortunate to attract a venture builder who became a cofounder (Box 6). Aside from funding, edtech startups expected investors to provide mentoring as part of business development support.

> We hope that investors can support our growth not only with the funds, but also with business assistance so we can be better off in running our business (Edtech no. 6).

Box 6: Benefits of Being Financed by a Venture Builder

One edtech founder said he was lucky to be supported by a venture builder. The owner of the venture builder then became his cofounder. They work closely together in nurturing the startup. The cofounder does regular monitoring and evaluation and ensures that the money is spent as planned and that the venture has no cash flow problems. The founder is an engineer and has no experience in management and finance. He said,

> Many founders choose their cofounders with the same background so they can share their thoughts easily. In my case, having a cofounder with a different background allows us to complement each other. So, it is really invaluable.

Apart from intensive mentoring, the venture builder also invites the founder to join the ecosystem where they can build networks and collaborate with other startups.

Source: Authors' in-depth interview with Edtech no. 4.

Government Programs and Regulations

For edtech founders, the government is an important actor in the ecosystem. Most informants said they have received support through incubation and acceleration programs, as mentioned earlier in this report. Most also appreciated the Kartu Prakerja—a program of the Coordinating Ministry for Economic Affairs—which funds training and support for the youth and others affected by the pandemic to upskill and enter the workforce. Participants can choose training provided by edtech enterprises, which is paid for by the program.

> It's good when the government launched the Kartu Prakerja Program and invited the edtech startups to participate and offered a partnership. I think it is very helpful to us (Edtech no. 1).

As enabler, the government plays an important role in implementing policies to support edtech startups. Table 10 summarizes how informants view some of the policy and program changes that would be beneficial.

Table 10: Perception of Better Regulations for Edtech Startups

Regulation	Perception
Permits and licenses	• Simplify permits and licenses, especially for online companies. • Improve foreign investment regulations.
Talent (labor)	• Expedite the development of a digital talent pool.
Tax and tariff	• Reduce tariffs on imported components. • Differentiate tax regulations between startups, small and medium-sized enterprises, and large corporations.
Others	• Explore the use of a regulatory sandbox for edtech startups.

Source: Authors.

Informants mentioned some issues related to the regulations, including the difficulties of registration.

> Startups receiving foreign funding automatically become foreign companies. The registration process of foreign companies is costly and takes a long time. This is the reason why registering in other countries becomes an option (Edtech no. 1).

There have been limits placed on foreign investment in the education sector, which have discouraged investors. As explained in Box 7, the restrictions have been modified and reduced over the years, but some restrictions remain and there is a strong perception that the education sector in Indonesia is not really open to foreign investors.

> In particular, the education sector is included in the Negative Investment List, limiting the ownership of foreign investors. This regulation hinders foreign investment in education (Edtech no. 2).

Box 7: The Struggle to Open the Education Sector to Foreign Investment

The education sector has long been considered too important to the nation's interests to be controlled by foreigners. It was not until 2007, when Law No. 25/2007 on Investment was issued, that the government slightly relaxed regulations on foreign investment in the sector. In the same year, the government issued Presidential Regulation No. 77/2007 on the Negative Investment List, which allowed foreign investors to hold up to 49% ownership stake in educational institutions (at any level: basic, high school, tertiary, and nonformal education).

Since then, regulations have evolved. In 2010, the government issued Presidential Regulation No. 36/2010, relaxing the requirements for the education sector from the previous Negative Investment List. However, the Supreme Court later canceled Law No. 9/2009 on Legal Entities of Education Institutions. The law was intended to make universities more independent and operate them as corporations. This cancellation resulted in the removal of the relaxation of foreign investment in the education sector as stipulated in Presidential Regulation No. 36/2010 on the Negative Investment List.

When the new administration started in 2014, President Joko Widodo showed strong commitment to give certainty to foreign investment. A significant shift took place with Presidential Regulation No. 44/2016 on the Investment Negative List, which opened the education sector to foreign investment under specific conditions. It stated that foreign investment in basic education should follow Law No. 20/2003 on the National Education System and in higher education Law No. 12/2012 on Higher Education. Foreign investment in the education sector must (i) be accredited by the National Accreditation Agency; (ii) partner with local educational institutions; and (iii) set up a nonprofit institution, namely a foundation. In 2021, under Law No. 11/2020, foreign investments can hold 100% ownership and be exempt from the first two requirements if the investment is located in a special economic area.

Sources: Gusman (2018); Directorate of Junior High School, Ministry of Education and Culture (2021); Wahyudi (2021).

In addition, investors prefer startups to be registered in Singapore. One informant from an edtech enterprise described his experience applying for follow-on investment. He was asked by the foreign investor to register his holding company in Singapore. Clearly, the foreign investors felt safer doing business within Singaporean regulations.

The government also treats startups and SMEs similarly in terms of licenses, labor regulations, and taxation. But edtech startups feel they should receive special treatment and that a regulatory sandbox—like the one used for fintech—is needed for edtech to determine how agile regulation should be applied to encourage innovation in the sector.

> It would be better if government allows the application of a regulatory sandbox so startups can test their innovation in a real setting (Edtech no. 1).

Product and Market

Informants mentioned product-market fit, market validation, and marketing strategy as important factors in startups' success. Some startups fail because they just duplicate a successful product from overseas without adapting it to local needs and end up with insufficient demand in the domestic market.

> When startups create a solution using technology without knowing the problem, they are prone to fail. We have to start with doing the research to understand what the problem is. Unfortunately, for many startups creating the technology is put first (Edtech no. 2).

Moreover, to gain market traction, startups must execute a good marketing strategy and be willing to innovate based on consumer demand.

> The products can't be separated from their marketing strategy. Feedback from the users is invaluable for product improvement (Edtech no. 6).

The Founders, the Team, and the Talent

The founder(s) and the team are important success factors. They determine the vision, the business model, and how to implement both. Moreover, team management and communication must be well managed and maintained to ensure stability and a unified purpose.

> The team is equally important, particularly the founder, as he/she holds the most strategic position and must have a good vision directing the development of the startup (Edtech no. 6).

Interestingly, the founder(s) and the team were mentioned by most informants as the main aspect of internal factors that determine the success of a startup.

Effects of the COVID-19 Pandemic

The impact of the COVID-19 pandemic was both positive and negative for edtech. On the positive side, some startups were able to expand their market as the pandemic created new opportunities. Edtech startups offering online education were given significant opportunities as educational activities moved online in both schools and universities.

> In a positive way, the pandemic forced education [to be] conducted online, so we had to adapt [to] the distance learning system or online system (Edtech no. 1).

It also gave a new opportunity for startups to expand their new business model.

> This pandemic made education activities to be conducted fully online, [so] we could get a big market and expand our business model into B2C, and not only B2B (Edtech no 6).

At the same time, the pandemic caused some startups to struggle with unstable conditions and lowered demand, jeopardizing the survival of their businesses. Some were thus encouraged (or forced) to rethink and redesign their business model and ensure better product-market fit.

> In the beginning of the pandemic, our market dropped drastically due to the sudden change (Edtech no. 1).

> Responding to the global pandemic, we changed our business model several times and put some business plans on hold (Edtech no. 4).

> We did the business pivot to increase business efficiency. We reduced our services from six features to three features that were needed most by the market (Edtech no. 5).

Challenges and Support Over the Life Cycle

Startups face different challenges at different phases of their development and need phase-specific support (Table 11). In the formation stage, startups must ensure that their products are most needed by the market. In this stage, startups begin to engage with potential customers.

> Startups have to work hard to get trust from the customers (Edtech no. 2).

Startups also rely on team members to develop the business. Sometimes startups have members with the same background, when in reality they need a variety of skills that complement each other. It is not necessarily beneficial for a team to have members with the same background. As one edtech startup noted,

> Startups whose team members are their fellows with the same background will more likely lack diversification in expertise (Edtech no. 4).

Table 11: Challenges in Each Phase and Support Needed in Edtech

Aspect of Challenges	Challenges in Each Phase			Support Needed
	Formation	**Stability**	**Scaling**	
Product	• Doing research to explore products needed by the market • Generating new products to meet market needs	• Improving the product • Achieving high growth and traction • Licensing administration	• Managing not only demand but also supply chains • Continue improving the product	• Tax deductions for startups • Product development support • Eased regulations on product licensing
Customer	• Get the trust of potential customers	• High marketing cost	• Exposure of the product	• Partnership with community • Business marketing support
Founder and team	• Forming a team with members who share a common background • Limited knowledge on business development	• Courage to take risks	• Must compete with unicorn startups to recruit new talent	• Business assistance support • Financial management support • Experience sharing with successors
Fund	• Grant • Competition prize	• Grant • Investment	• Investment • Lack of regulation for foreign investment	• Competition for startups • Networking with investors • Regulation on foreign investment

Source: Authors.

The challenge of funding at this stage is that startups are not yet able to win the trust of investors. Thus, they have to rely on grants or competition prizes.

> It's very difficult to get funds. Investors are difficult to convince at this stage (Edtech no. 1).

In the stability stage, the challenges are to improve the product, develop the market, and ensure traction.

> We have to refine the products and be brave to launch it to the market. In this case, sharing experiences with others is important (Edtech no. 4).

Growth is important to show that the startup will be a success and therefore a good investment.

> The growth rate has to be fulfilled [i.e., achieved] by the startups, and it's more difficult in the education sector than in e-commerce (Edtech no. 1).

Funding is needed not only to invest in equipment, conduct research, and pay expenses, but also for advertising so that potential customers are aware of the project.

> We need funding from investors to advertise the product. Even a good product has to be optimally advertised; or else, it will be unknown in the market (Edtech no. 5).

In the scaling stage, the challenges are even more complex. In particular, the startup must obtain the materials it needs to ramp up production. Otherwise, it will have difficulty meeting demand.

> Our production relies on overseas [suppliers] because it would be more expensive if we get the material directly from Indonesia (Edtech no. 4).

In terms of team capacity, startups need more talent to run the business. However, good talent prefers to work for unicorns instead of smaller startups. This was revealed by an edtech startup in the scaling stage.

> Finding talent which fits our needs [is important], but we have to compete with unicorn startups to get quality talent (Edtech no. 1).

Health and Healthtech

6

A unique feature of the healthtech market is that a large portion of the potential customer base consists of institutions, i.e., hospitals and clinics. Furthermore, a large share of the institutions is public, i.e., government owned and operated. Certainly, there is a market for goods and services purchased by individuals and households, but even some of these would come on the recommendation of doctors and health workers at institutions. Therefore, healthtech startups must cultivate and gain access to institutions to build their customer base. This can be a significant challenge.

The nature of the challenge depends very much on the orientation of the health-care system (curative versus preventive) and the current use of and openness to technology and innovation. It can be argued—and some of our informants did—that the health-care sector is not, or not yet, startup-friendly. This is firstly because it is not particularly open to technological innovation, and secondly because it focuses on curative care, whereas many healthtech solutions are preventive or promotive.

Therefore, the sector's business mindset may require systemic change and include affirmative policies toward a promotive and preventive approach. The government can encourage health sector stakeholders to develop such a mindset, which will encourage them to be more open to innovation from healthtech startups.

Incubators and Accelerators

In the healthtech sector, incubators and accelerators can play a significant role in supporting startups and connecting them with potential investors. Services can range from legal advice, mentorship, and guidance on pitching to providing seed funding in the form of grants or equity investments. It is important that programs are tailored to the needs of a startup at each development phase. Incubator and accelerator programs also provide links to networks. A program run by an academic institution, for-profit venture, or venture capital firm is expected to connect healthtech startups with their potential manufacturing partners, financiers, and more prominent startups to learn from.

> [The incubator] facilitates the startup to learn from more successful [startups] on communicating with investors and being updated on their growth. This kind of encouraging discussions could only be obtained from an informal talk during an [incubator] event (Healthtech no. 6).

Startups can benefit from a program, but not all need to join a program to be successful, and success is guaranteed because they joined.

> If you want to be successful, do not rely solely on an incubator. Unicorns such as Tokopedia and Bukalapak did not join any incubator yet they are considered successful. Moreover, that is because they went straight into business (Healthtech no. 7).

Our informants suggested areas in which incubators and accelerators have weaknesses and could be improved. Several startups suggested that advice was often not practical. Others felt that more sector-specific expertise was needed, as the health-care sector is complex and highly regulated.

> The quality is pretty good, but most of the programs are far too focused on theory rather than practical matters (Healthtech no. 9).

> No local incubators are focusing on healthtech. They [incubators] are more open to startups for digital communication. So, our needs have not been accommodated by any incubator or accelerator program in Indonesia. There is no effective and targeted support yet (Healthtech no. 12).

> There are no incubators that provide specific mentorship for the health sector. There are only business and economics mentors (Healthtech no. 8).

Like startups in other sectors, healthtech enterprises noted the unequal distribution of incubators and accelerators across regions. Most programs are concentrated in Java, especially Jakarta, although programs in the capital allow startups from other regions to join. Incubators and accelerators located outside of Java tend to lack experts to mentor their tenants.

> Our incubator brought in speakers from Jakarta for the program, [but we] had to wait up to a month. There is still a low supply of experts here (Healthtech no. 7).

> There are several incubators, but there are still [not] many programs. Local startups like ours are not much facilitated (Healthtech no. 11).

Some of the programs were perceived to be difficult for new startups to access, even when an incubator was geared toward early-phase startups. Incubators usually require a certain level of business traction, making it difficult for a startup in its formation phase to join. The registration process took quite a long time in some cases.

> The whole process took so long. We were waiting for approximately 6 months from online registration to announcement. During that time, we ran the bootstrapping process and even forgot that we had registered to join an incubation program (Healthtech no. 7).

Financing Institutions

Financing is an essential driver of healthtech development. Startups offer innovative tools or devices for improved health which take time to develop. The startup must build one or more prototypes, refine the product, and launch it to the market. This process is costly. Therefore, various financing options are needed for both working capital and long-term investment.

> Being able to generate investment is one of the top priorities for us since the research on our product's development is pricey (Healthtech no. 12).

The startups we interviewed found it challenging to access funding, especially equity investment. This is due to the lack of investors focusing on impact-based sectors like health care and most are only interested in profit and return. Another challenge is that financiers are not familiar with the sector, which also makes them hesitant to invest.

> Financing institutions in Indonesia are still focused on economic investment. So, startups that are likely to be given funding are assessed based on the return-on-investment scale matrix (Healthtech no. 3).

> Domestic investors do not have a strategic view of healthtech as an influential sector. I suppose that is why they are not interested in this sector just yet (Healthtech no. 12).

> Health is a strategic sector, but it is often difficult for investors to understand. It is hard to convince businessmen to understand that medical tourism is part of the creative economy (Healthtech no. 8).

For founders who have studied abroad, access to funding is easier. Such international and educational experiences give investors more confidence in a founder's ability to run a successful startup. The connections and networks between financiers and founders also influence funding decisions.

> Investors initially assess the startup based on their trust toward the founders and the market fit of their products. There are also many fellow founders whose startup products are not yet mature, but who have already received investment since the investors had already known them from their friendships and professional networks (Healthtech no. 9).

> Investors consider foreign university graduates, like [those from] Harvard, to be more trustworthy. Therefore, an international education background becomes an influential factor in getting funding (Healthtech no. 4).

The pandemic encouraged founders and their startups to develop digital health solutions. More startups in the market increased competition for funding and put small players at a disadvantage. Furthermore, access to finance is more challenging for healthtech startups outside of Java. The main reason is that they are not given sufficient support in networking with and pitching to investors.

> The ease for startups in the small cities to get investment differs from the ones located in the capital city. They [the financiers] did not specifically disclose the criteria, but seeing those who got investment, the criteria are mainly [that they demonstrate] market and business traction (Healthtech no. 11).

Government Programs

The government usually uses a pentahelix (five-party) collaboration model that includes academia, the private sector, the community, and the media. This approach is beneficial because it involves a wide range of stakeholders in discussions and collaborative projects. The government needs to—but does not always—recognize that startups are private businesses that are busy developing products and breaking into markets, and they may not have time for collaborative activities, especially those that do not generate business for the startup.

> We once had a collaborative program with the Ministry of Health. They were cooperative, but they wanted us to act as a nonprofit organization. We were hoping that there will be more win-win solutions because we are running a business (Healthtech no. 10).

The startups we interviewed had different experiences with the government's helpfulness. One multistakeholder activity was designed to put state-owned enterprises as the startups' manufacturing partners. However, one startup that participated felt that the government lacked awareness of business processes and approached production in a "bureaucratic way." Activities took too long, and public sector partners did not recognize the time-sensitive nature of startups and the ecosystem. Another startup, on the other hand, found connecting with the government in manufacturing essential.

We do not have sufficient funds to cover the production costs yet. Therefore, we built a partnership with one of the state-owned enterprises for the production process. They also handle the administration needed to import our primary commodity because they have the licensing (Healthtech no. 5).

Most government programs are centralized in Java, especially in the capital city. The lack of access to information about programs reduces the likelihood that a startup will join a program. In general, startups located outside of Java are less likely to participate in programs, even if they know about them. The startups that had access to government programs indicated that the programs still need improvement. Government support often focused on short-term events, although they targeted more than one-on-one business pitching. The lack of sustainability of the programs meant that there was insufficient support to take innovative and risk-taking startups to scale.

> Access for us in the small towns is difficult because most of the programs are centralized, so we only get to know any information from the group chat of the association (i.e., Association of Healthtech Indonesia). We get to know health regulations there. Direct access is limited. The government should be able to revive the local startup ecosystem here so that it will be more just (Healthtech no. 7).

There is also a lack of government programs specifically focused on the healthtech sector. Because it is a complex field, the lack of programs may be constraining the growth of startups and cause many to fail. Most programs focus on fintech and digital communication technology.

> We had to compete with non-healthtech startups offering innovations such as processed food, so the PPBT program was not focused at all. The judge is rather from [a] law or economics [background], which makes it hard for them to understand our services and give a relevant judgment. Most of the time, what is considered unique is a new food product instead of technology development (Healthtech no. 8).

Regulatory Environment

The health-care industry is subject to a complex set of regulations that govern almost every aspect and organization. This is to be expected, as it is a sensitive area involving the well-being of individuals and, indeed, matters of life and death. These regulations can make it difficult for new private sector players (startups) to join the system. There is a case for creating a regulatory sandbox for the sector that would allow startups to develop and test the regulation of new products and services.

A main concern relates to regulations that promote data interoperability, which allows two or more systems to exchange and use health information. With interoperability, health information (e.g., electronic medical records) can be exchanged and used simultaneously and securely from multiple locations by authorized users such as doctors, clinicians, and even healthtech startups. The lack of interoperability hampers regular data flow, but also limited data flow during the pandemic.

> Why does the government need to collect COVID-19 patient data one by one? That was ridiculous. [With data interoperability] the central government can see all the positive patients based on the data in their respective regions. Then what was the matter? Because there is no interoperability, no data goes straight through. Interoperability-related regulations do not exist, so there is never a separation of the metadata from the primary data (Healthtech no. 1).

Within the health-care sector, the storage, flow, and use of data can be an area where startups can offer solutions. These data are mostly patient information, so security (confidentiality) is a primary concern. Data interoperability is necessary as it allows for greater efficiency, especially in making decisions about treatment, through different parts of the care system, but must be designed to protect confidentiality. The current situation has not yet been able to strike the right balance between the need for data sharing and the importance of maintaining confidentiality.

> Integration [within and between] health facilities is difficult. If there is a long-established system, the providers are more reluctant to connect with a newer digital solution. What's being done is integration with the monopoly system rather than data interoperability. If a healthtech startup wants to assist the system through integrated connection, what will be connected without interoperability? [Can we] agree on which part of the information exchange [to modernize]? (Healthtech no. 1).

Data protection laws can also hinder some startups that require medical records. The draft Law on Personal Data Protection affects electronic medical records that were previously regulated by Ministry of Health Regulation No. 269/MENKES/PER/III/2008. Several informants in this study felt that the draft law is likely to have a profound impact on aspects of health-care and healthtech solutions. There is concern that the draft law will incorporate the General Data Protection Regulation (currently used in the European Union and considered a very strict privacy law), which designates electronic medical records as restricted data. This will constrain healthtech startups that need to share electronic medical records to better offer their solutions. Data interoperability may be reduced. Hence, regulating medical records as shareable data may be a better approach.

There could also be problems with business licenses not being available or suitable for laboratories and other private sector activities of startups.

> There is no business license yet to accommodate our alley. Now we are using industrial business licenses, even though we are running a laboratory instead of a factory. We have gone all out to register our business, but the current registration is not yet suitable. The rules for business license, exploratory research authorization, and data sharing protocols are not clear. Then, the cybersecurity policy from the government also has not been informed at all (Healthtech no. 12).

The Product, the Founder, and the Team

In healthtech, the product is important because it must not only satisfy the customer, but also guarantee safety and comply with other regulations. The startup can also try to develop a product that is not only profitable but also has great social impact. So, in the early stages, the focus is on product innovation, development, and impact. Refining the innovation remains important as the startup moves into the growth phase.

> Innovation is key in startup development. We need to consider whether this could solve a social problem or not (Healthtech no. 5).

Aside from the product, the startup team is also an influential internal factor. Most startups we interviewed agreed that financing institutions invest in the people behind the product, not the product itself. Therefore, founder and teamwork issues, such as compatibility over business vision and interest in the sector, are important as the startup grows and changes.

> Manpower is an important factor for the startup since most investors will be brought in by the people, not the business (Healthtech no. 10).

> The founder and cofounder of the startup need to have the same aim while also having the same interest in the industry (Healthtech no. 6).

> Team solidarity is the most important factor in building a successful startup. Different goals between the founders and the team members will lead to failure (Healthtech no. 11).

As a new entrepreneurial venture, a startup is prone to uncertainty in revenue streams and eventually, faces the "valley of death." The founders explained that most startups do not survive because the team members do not have an agreed, shared, and coherent business vision.

Moreover, the skills of the core team and other staff are important. Healthtech startups need to cover three areas: health, technology, and business. Different professional backgrounds are needed to create a team with the right skills mix. It is also helpful for founders to have a close network of knowledgeable people they can access to test ideas and learn about the latest developments in the industry.

> The founders and the team are the determining factors for a successful startup. However, the different backgrounds between founders and cofounders can also encourage the startup to be more dynamic. In our opinion, it would be better if the educational and professional backgrounds of the founder and cofounders are mixed (Healthtech no. 1).

Even when it is clear that the quality of the core team and other staff is important, it is often difficult to recruit and retain good talent, especially in towns and smaller cities.

> Unfortunately, this is still a one-person show since the turnover rate is quite high as some cofounders come and go. The team was lacking enthusiasm, thus making it difficult to convince them to work full time. Besides, they all had their respective [work] activities outside the startup (Healthtech no. 7).

> Since this is a small town, it is quite common for people to work somewhere stable once they finish their studies rather than build something new. It is harder to convince them of the business model that a startup offers (Healthtech no. 6).

Industry Association

The healthtech startup community plays a significant role in the regulatory advocacy related to the healthtech sector. The community is known for organizing private meetings and public dialogues with relevant stakeholders to advance the agenda related to telehealth and digital health regulations and the regulatory sandbox. The Association of Healthtech Indonesia plays an important role in this regard by providing information to its members and organizing stakeholder meetings, including the government.

> The support is beyond helpful. We, founders, finally found a platform to share and compare various decisions regarding our business sector. It is necessary to be able to build a network with each other (Healthtech no. 8).

> The most significant support is its Association of Healthtech Indonesia role in building a network with associates, business partners, ministries, and big corporations (Healthtech no. 6).

Location, Timing, and the COVID-19 Pandemic

Other important aspects are the location, timing, and the COVID-19 pandemic. The location of the startup's main office can be critical. Those located far from the capital, especially outside Java, often have a harder time gaining business traction because the market is not ready. The lack of technological literacy and infrastructure complicates efforts to scale up the business, including the difficulty finding suitable and committed talent and raising money.

> In a small town like this, the market is not yet ready for a startup. The population is pretty small, and most [people] are not technologically literate. One of our former team members moved to the capital city and built a startup with the same business model. His startup escalated in no time as the business traction increased rapidly (Healthtech no. 11).

> The geographic aspect highly affects startups. It played a big role in the main costs and resources. We chose to have our main office here in this city because the talent is easier to find. While we also opened an office in the capital city because it is easier to access the market and do fundraising (Healthtech no. 10).

The timing of the business (or product launch) is also essential, considering the need to traverse the "valley of death." This refers to the difficulty of sustaining the business while cash flow is negative in the early phase. To overcome this problem, healthtech startups try to obtain investment, loans, and grants to cover operating costs while they are not yet generating revenue.

> Timing is also critical and definitive. Regarding timing, the shortcut is often to find as much funding as possible to last until the time comes (i.e., reaching the "valley of death" curve). We need to set the main goals as clear as possible so we can survive and pivot while still being on track (Healthtech no. 1).

In a strange way, the pandemic has been the next "big thing" for healthtech startups. On the one hand, it challenged the communication flow between them and potential investors. It also created obstacles in maintaining partnerships with health workers to provide in-house health-care services. On the other hand, the pandemic created a situation in which health-care providers were forced to consider adopting digital solutions.

> We need to admit that the pandemic could bring some benefits to healthtech startups. It's now easier to work with hospitals. I suppose that they have become more open to collaboration with digital sectors. Indeed, the icebergs have started to melt. One of them is that people are forced to change because of the pandemic (Healthtech no. 6).

Challenges and Support Needed in Each Phase

Based on self-assessment, the healthtech startups we interviewed consist of one startup in the formation phase, one in the stability phase, two between the stability and scaling phases, and seven in the scaling phase. Each phase of development presents different challenges for startups (Table 12). The challenges in the ecosystem are mainly related to the product, founder, and funding. Meanwhile, the challenges in the health sector are related to health-care providers and current regulations.

Table 12: Challenges in Each Phase and Support Needed in Healthtech

Aspect of Challenges		Challenges in Each Phase			Support Needed
		Formation	Stability	Scaling	
Startup	Product	Doing research	Validation, market fit	Traction	Consumer education, market access
	Founder/team	Talent	Churn rate	Skill	Mentorship, sustainable assistance
	Fund	Grant, award	Grant, investment	Investment	Varied financing options, prototyping grant from the government
Health	Health-care provider	–	Mindset	Network	Consumer education, including affirmative policy and regulation
	Health regulations	–	Market entry	Data interoperability	Regulatory sandbox, ease of doing business

Source: Authors.

Formation Phase

In this phase, healthtech startups found it challenging to develop their initial ideas. The common practice for these startups was to become part of an incubator or accelerator program to receive business mentorship and other assistance. However, it was quite a challenge to find a program that would provide them with a combination of mentors with expertise in business, tech, and health.

Startups need to test and trial their products in this phase because an unsafe product could jeopardize the life of a user. In the health sector, exploratory research requires product research authorization, which can be difficult to obtain. This challenge particularly affects startups that are developing tools and devices for improved health.

> For genetic research, it is important to have authorization for exploratory research because we need to collect samples. So, our business administration was listed under industrial business license with a research and development unit. Later, when our startup is audited, there will only

be a research and development unit, while the industrial [business] will not exist. This is our strategy because our business model was not accommodated in regulations (Healthtech no. 12).

The startups that focus on digital health and telehealth services are mainly challenged by compliance with rules and regulations related to the use of data and technology. In Indonesia, regulations related to these aspects are still in a gray area. Regulations that have a profound impact on healthtech startups include the management of private data centers based on Government Regulation No. 71/2019 on the Implementation of Electronic Systems and Transactions, the draft Personal Data Protection Bill, and the National Strategy for Artificial Intelligence introduced in August 2020. The resulting uncertainty has undermined the certainty founders need to develop their healthtech startups.

> Our AI [artificial intelligence]-based services were completely discontinued because the existing regulations did not exist for it. In Indonesia, the discussion about storing patient data is still translated as medical records that must be stored in health facilities. How many hospitals do we have to work with to store the data? (Healthtech no. 3).

This uncertainty makes talented individuals and other experts reluctant to participate in health-care startups. The reluctance stems from the common perception that a startup is a high-risk business model with high failure and low growth rates. It is seen as risky especially in areas where people are unfamiliar with the daily use of digital tech. The relatively high market risk creates a poor business image, making talent recruitment and willingness to work full-time key issues.

Access to grants through awards and incubator and accelerator programs has also been a major challenge. The main reason for this is that the startup ecosystem, both locally and nationally, is unfamiliar with the healthtech sector. The startup founders we interviewed were concerned about being put in the same category with startups from other sectors. They pointed out that healthtech has more specific challenges to overcome, such as patient data security protocols and the medical device production process. The immense gap between startups in a highly regulated landscape like healthtech and startups from more relaxed sectors like food and beverage was perceived as a reason for the need for affirmative action from stakeholders.

Therefore, a regulatory sandbox that acts as a "safe space" for healthtech startups to test new solutions under certain conditions and limitations is urgently needed. Once the regulatory landscape is clearer, prototyping grants to build, e.g., for medical devices, will be useful in the formation stage.

Stability Stage

In the stability stage, startups face new changes. A major problem, highlighted above, is the sector's focus on curative and rehabilitative solutions rather than of preventive or promotional ones. Startups producing for the latter find that institutions and medical personnel are reluctant to adopt their solutions.

Many doctors, administrators, and health-care workers are still unfamiliar with new technologies that could be used in their institutions. There is also a widespread lack of readiness to trust digital health-care services and technological innovations to improve health. Therefore, digital transformation and the use of healthtech in the complex field of health care may take time.

> The most difficult challenges have been trying to reach local hospitals and health centers. Most hospitals are not yet friendly to new technology, with the exception of the big private hospitals, which are usually more open-minded and more willing to update their health systems. Government health-care facilities are still outdated. Management should change this understanding (Healthtech no. 4).

Furthermore, most health-care providers emphasize cure rather than prevention. The focus on providing curative and rehabilitative health-care services is accompanied by a reluctance to adopt new, digital solutions for prevention. Healthtech startups with preventive or promotional solutions face difficulty in having them adopted by health-care professionals and institutions.

> If we look at government health facilities, such as public health centers, they offer curative rather than promotive services. They focus more on purchasing medicines and preparing referrals. Promotive services are still provided, but they are not a priority, even though that is [should be] their main job. This has negative implications for us. Our startup promotes a preventive approach, which makes it harder for us to penetrate health-care facilities, even though our product could significantly help to prevent various diseases (Healthtech no. 5).

Another challenge for startups in health is the regulation of market entry. The entire process of business licensing, market authorization, and intellectual property patenting can take months or years. Startups with considerably more initial capital can hire consultants to tackle these issues, but most startups did not have the funds for such an approach. Without proper legal documents, product validation to meet customer demands is not possible.

Licensing regulations are also a supporting factor for startup development. This is because of the difficulty in validating the product when the license has not yet been registered. Therefore, licensing can be a challenge for health startups in Indonesia (Healthtech no. 9).

Financing at this stage should come from grants or equity investment. Securing a loan, even with a low interest rate, is not usually possible because startups cannot show sufficient income to service the loan. The typical mechanism for startups to generate investment is to pitch to investors. However, since investors are not familiar with healthtech, it is difficult for startups to stand out during multisector business pitching events.

Problems securing financing lead to difficulties in attracting and retaining talented employees with high salary expectations. As a compromise, startups can offer a stock option plan that allows the employee to own a portion of the company's stock. Of course, the employee must be willing to bet on the startup's success. However, this mechanism is generally not attractive enough to retain employees and is not often offered in Indonesia.

Many startup employees leave for a full-time position in a stable company. Meanwhile, some team members leave to develop a similar startup in another area with a more significant market, such as Jakarta. The startups we interviewed mentioned that they need more varied financing options to solve this problem. Aside from current financing sources, such as grants and equity investment, other options like a government loan with low or no interest rates and long repayment terms were needed.

> One of our former team members moved to Jakarta. Using the knowledge he had learned from our startup, he built a similar startup, and it developed well ahead of ours. In metropolitan areas like the capital city, startups automatically increase business traction rapidly, whereas in our area, finding a market for startups is difficult (Healthtech no. 11).

Scaling Phase

In the scaling phase, healthtech startups rely heavily on innovation, demand, and affordability of their products. Traction means that the startup has measurable demand that it can use to convince investors. Innovation, in turn, requires that more experts be part of the team. For startups at this phase, hiring full-time employees is quite a challenge because of the cost. This challenge stems from various factors, such as competition from other brands and insufficient funding. As a result, there is a shortage of skilled individuals willing to work full-time in healthtech startups.

The initial founders were no longer directly involved. It was also difficult to find people willing to work full time in a startup and who have the required skills. There was a lack of talent, so our chief technology officer had to struggle alone. At the time of mobile application development, we found it difficult due to the lack of talent (Healthtech no. 11).

Furthermore, scaling also means expanding the customer base. For many healthtech startups, this means getting more hospitals and clinics to adopt their products or recommend them to patients. The common practice for healthtech startups is to expand their networks to build partnerships with health-care providers.

We currently try to approach big health facilities. So far, we were able to run the business because I am a lecturer and a doctor with a medical license in three different hospitals. So, these three places can be used for our promotion and partnership (Healthtech no. 8).

Environment, Climate Change, and Greentech

7

Cleantech is a broad concept that encompasses technologies to reduce society's impact on the physical ecosystem. It provides environmentally friendly solutions to mitigate and adapt to climate change. There is no agreement on what subsectors or activities it can encompass, but it generally includes clean energy, solid and liquid waste management, green materials, environmental quality (water, air, and soil), green transport, and sustainable farming (Webb, Cruz, and Walsh 2017; Jensen, Lööf, and Stephan 2020).[27]

We interviewed 12 startups in the energy (4) and waste (8) sectors. These startups operate in different subsectors and employ different business models. In the energy sector, two startups offer solar energy solutions and the other two offer energy efficiency products. In the waste sector, two startups offer waste processing services, two focus on bioprocessing organic waste (and selling the products derived from it), and one each provides waste collection, technologies to support waste collection, a platform that connects waste banks and other waste management entities, and the creation of building materials from recycled materials.

Based on a self-assessment, one startup was in the formation stage, three were in the stability stage, one was between stability and scaling, and seven were in the scaling stage. The average age was 4.5 years. The interviewed startups were all located in urban areas: nine in Greater Jakarta and one each in Bali, Yogyakarta, and Pontianak, the latter being the only startup outside of Java and Bali.

Cleantech startups feel there is ample room for improvement in the performance of each actor in the ecosystem. This section focuses on the startups' perception of these actors.

---

[27] The definition of cleantech and the subsectors it encapsulates is a topic of continued debate (Caprotti 2016).

Incubators and Accelerators

All but 1 of the 12 startups we interviewed participated in an incubator or accelerator program, and 7 had participated in more than one. The programs in which our startup informants participated were mostly local, but there were also several startups that participated in international programs. Programs varied in duration, scope, and support provided, but generally provided courses on basic business skills (e.g., leadership, marketing and communications, business planning, business strategy), business support (e.g., legal, licenses and permit assistance), mentoring, access to networks (e.g., government stakeholders, investors), and access to markets (e.g., industry partners, product showcase events). Some programs also provided financial support.

Incubators and accelerators can support the success of startups by providing them with the basic knowledge needed for growth and development. Their support is especially helpful if the founder does not have a business education or background, but comes from the tech side. Although these programs are generally beneficial, one startup said that the development of a startup does not depend on them; it all depends on the startup's product and how the startup can make the most of it. Without a good product, even the best incubator or accelerator cannot lead the startup to success.

> For the ecosystem itself, startup development does not depend on accelerators, but on the products we sell. If the product fits the needs, it will generate revenue, but if the product is not as good as [i.e., appropriate for] the needs, the accelerator can not fix that. The aim of the accelerator is more to be sure. For example, if we want to work with the government, we join, if we want to connect with our venture capital, we join (Cleantech no. 9).

Most startups feel that the number of incubators and accelerators available in Indonesia is sufficient relative to the number of startups. However, it can be difficult to gain entry to an incubator or accelerator program because the selection standards are high. Several informants pointed out that there are not many incubators and accelerators that accept early-stage startups. Instead, they are more likely to accept startups that already have a clear product, traction, and cash flow, especially if the program offers funding as part of the support package.

> To be able to join the program, startups must meet certain standards. So there are enough accelerators and incubators, but the quality of startups that are accepted into the program is key, because there is a selection process (Cleantech no. 9).

Incubators and accelerators are not interested in new startups, but in those that have a cash flow and are already presentable—even if they [incubators and accelerators] are needed when startups are still in their early stages (Cleantech no. 7).

The startups' perception of quality is varied. All startups noted that they benefited from participating in the available programs. Some startups felt that the quality and support provided by the programs were good and met their development needs. Being able to participate in these programs helped them to progress to the next level. However, there were also several caveats mentioned by startups, notably the unequal distribution of programs across the country, the effectiveness of some programs, and the lack of continuity (i.e., follow-up support) after the startup graduates.

First, although startups generally agree that the number of incubators and accelerators is sufficient, some startups said that programs are unevenly distributed. High-quality programs are concentrated in metropolitan cities and are particularly limited to Jakarta, Bandung, and Yogyakarta. As a result, there are few incubators in other regions. This is a challenge especially for startups outside the large cities.

> The number of incubators and accelerators nationally is sufficient, but the distribution is not even and the quality of incubators and accelerators in the regions is not as good as in big cities (Cleantech no. 5).

Second, the quality of the programs still has room for improvement. One startup said that the support provided is not targeted to the needs of each startup, as most programs structure their material in a generalized, top–down approach.

> Although the supply is large, sometimes the quality does not match what the startup needs. The problem is that some processes are not suitable for certain startups. Therefore, the program is not as effective (Cleantech no. 10).

Another informant said that the themes and topics presented were "standard" and that the startup had already learned them before. Also, the program felt more like motivation sessions.

> In terms of quality, the themes discussed by the incubator [or] accelerator are still very standard, mostly motivational sessions that we have already been through before (Cleantech no. 5).

In addition to business coaching, some startups said that the programs would be more effective if they supported access to funding, whether directly through the program itself or through the networking that the programs could offer startups.

> A session that is needed is one that can connect [us] with investors. We have done it, but it was not optimal because only local people were invited (Cleantech no. 5).

> An effective incubator [or] accelerator scheme, apart from offering a mentor, should also provide funding (Cleantech no. 1).

Third, startups felt that the programs lacked continuity because there was no substantial follow-up after the startups graduated. Not much thought was given to what happens next. After finishing a program, startups are assumed to be able to implement what they have learned, even though there is an obvious gap between theory and practice. In their development and especially through trial and error, startups need feedback. Therefore, some startups felt that an ideal program should have a post-graduation follow-up mechanism planned from the beginning. After participants graduate, programs should continue to monitor and mentor the startups' development for some time to ensure that the startups are able to thrive independently.

> In terms of the quality of incubator [or] accelerator support, startups have been able to get a lot of insights, but the weakness of the programs is that they [do not provide continuous support]. After leaving a program, we were considered and assumed to be able to [survive] despite the differences between theory and practice in different fields. Meanwhile, startups need feedback on the challenges [they face] in the field (Cleantech no. 3).

In addition, several startups raised the issue of the lack of cleantech-focused programs, or at least the availability of mentors with expertise in the cleantech sector within general incubator programs. A narrow definition, or perhaps even a low awareness, of what cleantech encapsulates has hampered the development of the sector and the growth of ecosystem players in Indonesia. For example, an informant felt that for many people, cleantech is synonymous with clean energy—and indeed, the only cleantech-focused incubator or accelerator program in Indonesia is only available to energy startups. This lack of specificity and expertise in the programs can limit the possibilities for cleantech startups to thrive.

> There is no specialized incubator [or] accelerator for the cleantech sector, so cleantech startups have to enter general incubators [or] accelerators. Maybe [people think] cleantech is just clean energy, but in reality it can cover other environmental issues, so there should be other specialized incubators (Cleantech no. 2).

Many startups do not survive, perhaps because incubators do not understand the startup sector. For example, they do not understand the cleantech sector, or they consider cleantech the same as the e-commerce sector. In fact, the specific sector of deep tech needs to be well understood (Cleantech no. 10).

An ideal incubator or accelerator program should not only support the business aspect of startups, but also the sector aspect. On the business side, most startups suggest that better access to funding and networking with investors are needed, as well as greater program sustainability with follow-up after graduation. To support the sectoral aspect, more specific cleantech incubators and accelerators could be promoted, as well as specialized mentors.

Financing Institution

All but 1 of the 12 cleantech startups interviewed had passed the formation stage. However, each of them had active cash flow. In addition to bootstrapping and revenue, all startups had received funding from at least one external source. Two startups had received funding from an angel investor, one had received funding from a venture capital fund, and others had received funding in the form of competition prize money and/or grants.

Several interviewees noted the importance of financing as a critical factor in the success of startups. Sufficient financing can help startups run their operations optimally, so that team members can focus on doing their best for the venture. Two startups highlighted the importance of financing in the early stages to cover R&D and talent recruitment costs. One startup added that besides funding, what investors offer, such as guidance and access to networks, is also important for startups. One startup mentioned that investors need to better understand the startup's conditions and not always push for growth or immediate revenue.

Although all startups have received external funding in one way or another, startups generally agreed that fundraising is difficult. Several are currently considering seeking funding from angel investors but are unable to approach any. This is a particular challenge for startups outside of Java. One startup tried to apply for funding from venture capital funds but failed because its financial calculations did not meet the funds' criteria.

> We have not had any angel investors and we have never applied, because angel investors can be approached [usually] through events that are held once a year, so we can not contact them every time (Cleantech no. 8).

> In our region, few are willing to invest in technology. Until now, we have not had any angel investors, but after discussions with several angel investors, they are still not sure about the technology business, especially in this region and especially because we are service-based (Cleantech no. 5).

> So far, we have not had any investors from VC [venture capital funds]. I have tried several times, but it seems that the business calculations have not matched. Regarding the criteria for investors, there has been no detailed calculation, because we focus more on digital platforms and the business calculation is not very attractive (Cleantech no. 4).

In terms of investment criteria, some startups noted that not all startups have a clear idea of what investors' criteria are and what responsibilities they must fulfill after receiving funding. Ideally, startups should be on a relatively stable footing before receiving funding, especially for equity. Both parties involved in the deal should agree on the criteria. For example, one startup said that it is difficult to agree on the share of equity given to the investor. Investors tend to ask for a higher percentage to gain dominance, but the capital they offer is not that large. Startups that are in a pinch may agree to these terms, but if startups can survive without the investment, they will choose to bootstrap instead of giving over a large portion of their ownership at a premature stage. Therefore, before seeking commercial funding, most startups go the incubator and accelerator route or enter competitions to develop first.

> In terms of what incentive could be given so that investors are willing to invest in cleantech, we are also not clear about what they look for. So, we don't know what indicator they are using. Maybe we need to search for that data (Cleantech no. 10).

> [To startups, financiers say] 'this must be nurtured first, through coaching and further development,' then we [financing institutions] can entrust the money and funding (Cleantech no. 4).

> The distribution of shares [to investors] is necessary, but we must be careful and see with whom we share the shares. The funding institution must be able to let us grow, and not [be] those who just want the shares (Cleantech no. 1).

Some informants believe that organic growth is the ideal and only way for startups to grow sustainably, but other informants also said that investment is necessary for startups to scale. When startups decide to seek funding, they consider other factors besides the investment amount. One startup rejected an offer because the financing scheme did not meet its own requirements. Startups also prefer investors who have experience with similar startups, especially in the same sector, and who can provide them with sector-related insights, business advice, and networking. Indeed, what the financing institution can offer in addition to funding is a factor that startups consider. One startup said that when a cleantech startup succeeds in getting funding from an angel investor, for example, it means they have agreed on a shared vision and mission.

> The reason we chose that particular VC is because we needed someone behind that VC to help us grow, since they have a lot of experience with Indonesian startups. We want to get insights from the people behind the VC as we move to the next round of funding (Cleantech no. 2).

> Some VC and international capital have shown their interest, but [from] our evaluations, we did not feel comfortable with their funding scheme (Cleantech no. 3).

Startups in the cleantech sector felt that funding for cleantech is limited. This is because the sector is still seen as unattractive—risk is high and return on investment takes a long time.

> For the waste management and sustainability sector, funding is still minimal because it is quite risky and it takes a long time to get a return on capital. In the end it all depends on how profitable the business is (Cleantech no. 9).

> Access to funding in the cleantech sector has been difficult, especially before 2018. After 2018, it was more open, and in 2020–2021 there were more varied options as the sector was perceived as fresh and promising. However, the niche is still relatively narrow, such as for plastics (Cleantech no. 1).

Startups said that an ideal form of financing would be impact investments that include a grant aspect because cleantech, like other impact sectors, requires a longer period to generate a return. The grant portion of the scheme would serve as initial funding to support the startup until it can develop a proven model. Additional funding could be provided in the form of equity to ensure the sustainability of the business. However, implementing impact investments in Indonesia is still relatively difficult due to a lack of standards for impact sustainability, which makes tracking impact difficult.

> Many investments in the form of impact [do not] enter Indonesia because the startups that are being considered to receive investment are not ready. For example, there are standards such as the GRI [Global Reporting Initiative] about which Indonesian startups are relatively unaware of. Regarding impact investment, investors usually ask startups to showcase

the sustainability of their impact: can it be measured and how is it measured? Most of the time, cleantech startups have difficulty answering such questions because they are not familiar with them (Cleantech no. 2).

An effective funding scheme has an impact side to it and must have a form of grant, because in the impact sector, returns require quite a long time. The grant serves as a boost at the beginning to get a proven model. In addition, there also needs to be a form of investment to make it sustainable. Through grants we do not need to give up shares, and we can develop certain products and focus more on them, but the difficulty is that there is no continuity (Cleantech no. 1).

Government

Government was most frequently cited by cleantech startups as a key factor for success. Three roles of government were highlighted: (i) as a partner and collaborator, (ii) as a provider of opportunities for startups, and (iii) as a regulator.

First, the government's large role in the cleantech and environment sectors makes it an important stakeholder for startups to collaborate with. Furthermore, the government has the power to promote and increase public awareness, not only of the issue, but also of the products and services that startups offer.

Collaboration with the government is important because the government has the power to promote and increase public awareness of our products (Cleantech no. 12).

Second, the government can support startups by providing programs and competitions, offering space for startups to showcase their products, and allowing startups to participate in government tenders. Third, as a regulator, the government has the power to create a supportive regulatory environment.

Although not all startups interviewed participated in government programs, almost all informants were familiar with the government's role in the startup ecosystem, namely through programs, policies, regulations, and as a partner. Four of the 12 startups interviewed had participated in a government program for startups, while three other startups from the waste subsector had actively worked with government stakeholders.

Most startups felt that government support was sufficient, as the programs were similar to those typically offered by incubators and accelerators. However, they also felt that there were better programs outside of government programs.

One informant said that the CPPBT and PPBT programs do not cater to the specific needs of startups. Furthermore, government programs often lack sustainability. The government should continue to collaborate with incubators and accelerators as this would provide a more targeted approach than government programs being executed by government agencies.

> Government support has been effective because through this program we were able to make contacts, reach a wider market, share knowledge, and develop our business (Cleantech no. 9).

> Through government support, startups received many insights, but the weakness of the programs is that they did not provide sustained support (Cleantech no. 5).

Collaboration with the government was actively sought by three startups from the waste subsector, as the government is the most important stakeholder in waste management. These startups preferred to partner with the government rather than become a competitor. They offered their expertise and added value to improve government waste management services or fill gaps that the government could not reach. However, one startup mentioned that given the fast pace of startups, the government could be quicker and less complicated in providing support.

> The ideal government support would be in the form of collaboration between startups and the government as well as access to the government where we can be a digital solutions provider (Cleantech no. 4).

> We work closely with the government because when we talk about competitors in this area, the main competitor is the government because they also provide waste transportation services, but they cannot reach the entire region, and there are certain segments they cannot reach. For example, here they have a monopoly on hotels, so we shouldn't take the hotels (Cleantech no. 5).

Overall, there is still no organized support for the cleantech sector and its startups, but one startup said that the government has many initiatives planned and approached them.

> There is currently no support for the cleantech sector, but there is a lot planned. The government intends to create programs and embrace startups, especially in the cleantech sector. Whether the government's support for the cleantech sector is sufficient or not, I do not know for sure. However, I assume that [support for] non-cleantech will be greater (Cleantech no. 6).

The government does not need to be the executor of programs to develop startups, but instead can position itself as a collaborator to help startups get a foothold in the market, especially because cleantech is a nascent sector.

Regulations

Informants raised more issues related to sectoral regulations (water and energy) than to business regulations. The key issues include the lack of clear sectoral regulations and their full and efficient implementation. Regulations can increase public awareness and create incentives for customers to use products and services from startups.

According to informants, current regulations are neither too discouraging nor sufficiently encouraging, and many aspects are still rather gray. Two informants mentioned the importance of regulatory clarity, and that regulations should not restrict a startup's growth too much. Sometimes the government has failed to anticipate or quickly adapt to developments in the startup industry, resulting in reactive and excessive regulations. Given the fast pace at which the startup industry operates, regulations should be implemented more quickly. The government needs to be aware of and continuously monitor what is currently happening in the industry and how far it has come.

> The ideal role of the government is to make correct and clear regulations, but also not to oppose the development of startups. It is not right to issue regulations that are reactive and make it difficult for startups. Sometimes the government moves way too slowly. I feel that we as startups are already 5–10 years ahead of the government in terms of innovation. The government should be monitoring the field so they know what is happening and where it is going (Cleantech no. 1).

The Ministry of Energy and Mineral Resources has issued regulations to promote the use of renewables as part of the nation's energy mix. An example provided by an informant was the green building regulation, which promotes the use of solar panels. However, there are no clear implementation guidelines for this regulation and no funding scheme for green building. Regulations also need to raise public awareness and incentivize customers to use energy-saving or renewable energy products offered by startups.

> There are no penalties for energy-intensive industries [businesses] that do not meet the energy conservation standard under Government Regulation No. 70/2009 on Energy Conservation. So, the industry lacks enthusiasm to report on its energy management program and how much energy has been saved. Incentives [and] penalties are needed in the regulation of energy conservation (Cleantech no. 3).

For the waste sector, there are several layers of regulatory issues compiled from the informant interviews. First, enforcement of regulations and standards for waste management is still low. Startups in this field therefore often operate in a gray area. For example, startups that offer waste management services do not have permits because there is no framework that requires them. While this may seem to ease administrative processes, it can be a double-edged sword, because without a permit, it is more difficult to gain the trust of customers and collaborate with other stakeholders in waste management processes.

> Until now, we do not have a permit because the government does not have regulations for waste processing. The government is confused about the classification of permits (Cleantech no. 8).

> The regulations need to be very clear. That way, the community can actually receive the appropriate service, because if there are no regulations, it becomes a bit chaotic and messy. Some communities don't get any waste management at all, and eventually they just ride motorbikes to dump [their waste] into the river because they do not know how to access waste management services. So, clearer regulations are needed. The main factor is law enforcement, because sometimes with regulations in Indonesia... there are already paper documents, but there is no implementation on the ground due to a lack of legal supervision and monitoring—that should go hand in hand (Cleantech no. 2).

Second, because the government currently serves as both the regulator and the executor of waste management, one informant said that the government may view startups as competitors and might be less inclined to collaborate. Meanwhile, startups in the sector continue to grow as there is a clear need for more waste management services.

> Since the government is also the executor, it views startups in the waste management field as competitors. Currently, there are no startups that are guided by the government—there are many garbage pick-up apps, but even in the capital city, garbage collection is still done manually [without apps], even though there are so many application-based digital start-ups for waste collection. Unfortunately, the government is not paying attention to this (Cleantech no. 5).

> The government needs to be assertive in waste regulation because implementation is not happening. The regulations are in place, but the role of the government is not fulfilled. Indeed, the government should only act as a regulator, not as an executor; the government [would] provide a broad stage for startups or business actors in the environment sector to

act as executors. But, currently in Indonesia, the government plays only a secondary role, so waste is not managed properly (Cleantech no. 7).

Third, since waste management is a regional affair, startups must engage with regional governments and deal with different regional regulations when working in multiple regions. Decentralized regulations pose a challenge in several ways, from obtaining permits to inconsistent waste policies. This challenge was raised by some informants whose startups operated in several regions or were planning to expand into other regions.

> Decentralized regulation is a challenge because it depends on the regional leadership. If the regional head thinks that this [waste] is a priority issue, it is usually better. However, if the head of the region changes, including the head of the department, the program must start all over again, so it becomes ineffective, and the Ministry of Environment and Forestry has no authority. The central ministry has better capacity than the regional government because local governments change quickly and not everyone in the local environment office understands environmental issues. So there is room for more political will (Cleantech no. 2).

Like the energy sector, informants from the waste sector highlighted a lack of regulations to incentivize the public to manage waste properly. Informants said that it would be very helpful if the government could enact regulations that encourage the use of eco-friendly goods; implement waste management at the household and commercial levels; and improve public education and socialization on waste issues. The informants also hoped that the government could be more open to collaborate with the private sector and delegate some of the waste management processes to startups.

> In terms of educating the public, the government should issue regulations for community socialization to sort waste and delegate the private sector as the executor. The government must be able to become a partner and work hand in hand with the private sector or other ecosystems. Regulations can also take the form of incentives and punishment so that people [will] want to sort their waste. In the current waste collection system, this becomes an obstacle because people are often disappointed when the waste they sort is mixed again. So this regulation also needs to be improved (Cleantech no. 7).

Therefore, more supportive regulations are needed to (i) promote use of startups' products and services through incentives and disincentives (e.g., encourage people to switch to renewable energy, be more mindful of energy use, manage their waste more responsibly, etc.); and (ii) promote collaboration.

On business regulations, most informants did not think business permits and licensing were a problem. They said that the current system and regulations have made these processes much easier. However, some informants spoke of issues they had with the tax system and regulations. From an administrative perspective, it is still difficult for startups to manage taxes online because of the complicated mechanisms involved. Therefore, startups go directly to the tax office, which is time-consuming. Startups believe that there should be tax relief mechanisms to ensure that new and growing startups are not burdened by the taxes imposed on them. Since startups are less financially stable than conventional businesses, some startups felt it was a burden to be treated the same way for tax purposes.

Product

To be successful, startups must create products with effective market fit. The products that startups offer must have a clear positioning of what problems they solve. Products that are based only on the founder's idea and ego will not attract customers. Even if there is a clear benefit to customers, startups must build people's trust in the product and willingness to use it. Especially with cleantech products, getting customers to switch from conventional products to innovative and environmentally friendly products is a major challenge.

> The product is important because we have to make products that people want and need, not something we have to force on the market. Usually there are many founders who develop very sophisticated technologies, but when they are offered to the market, people are not interested and have no need for them (Cleantech no. 1).

Good product-market fit also requires a price point that is both affordable and generates sufficient revenues.

Founders and Teams

The expertise and drive of the founders and core team were cited as key factors by all the cleantech startups we interviewed. Founders provide the core ideas of the startup and must have vision, determination, and perseverance to bring the ideas to fruition. Founders lead their startups in navigating markets and the ecosystem and attracting partners and investors. Since the involvement of the founder is very important, he or she must commit to the startup full-time.

> Founders and cofounders are very important, from persistence to idea to execution. Moreover, in Indonesia the execution is still low [weak]; there are ideas but no execution (Cleantech no. 6).

The first factor for the success of a startup is the consistency of the founder. Founders must have a strong desire regarding the issue because startups begin with solutions to real problems. For example, if the founder is inconsistent from the beginning or does not have a strong desire for the issue, [he or she] can only see it from the business side; if there is no result, it will not continue (Cleantech no. 2).

While the founder is important, a startup is seldom a one-person act and is still based on a team, even if it starts small. A startup needs a shared vision and mission for all members of the team. A shared vision and mission nurtures team solidarity and ensures cooperation and collaboration among members.

An important internal factor for the success of a startup is team solidarity. The biggest internal challenge for startups is building cooperation among members [or] founders to achieve the same vision, because from there we can determine how to achieve the vision, the management of the startup itself, and so on (Cleantech no. 2).

The founders and team members should come from different backgrounds and have different expertise. In this way, they can complement each other.

Founders and team must be able to complement each other, must be willing to develop and learn from each other (Cleantech no. 9).

Internal factors that determine the success of the most dominant startups are the persistence of a strong founder and team. Thus, the founder and the team are the most determinant [factors], regardless of the ecosystem (Cleantech no. 3).

Communities (Cleantech Community and Startup Community)

When asked about the role of communities, several startups mentioned their importance for information and talent. Through communities, startups get information and stay updated on markets, products, forums, and available talent.

Community has an important role. I belong to the startup community, not specifically the cleantech community. The community plays an important role for information, so we stay updated. One of the roles of the community is related to talent, usually we get talent from the community where people are already aware (Cleantech no. 1).

Communities are not necessarily sector-specific, and in fact there are not many cleantech-focused community organizations. For the waste sector, this is now being addressed. For the energy sector, Indonesia has a solar energy association that actively advocates for solar power policies and regulations.

The COVID-19 Pandemic

The pandemic had a particularly negative impact on the cleantech sector, causing a drop in demand or a disruption in the supply chain. Some startups suspended operations for some time and canceled expansion plans.

> The pandemic has left quite an impact. Many of our clients did not operate, especially restaurants; for 3–6 months they did not do business at all. Therefore, the amount of waste has decreased because we usually transport garbage from commercial areas. The solution was to try to collect more waste from households. It is more difficult [to collect from households] because not every household is aware of waste management's significance. In addition, we previously did waste management at events, [but they] were canceled (Cleantech no. 2).

> It was hard to find trash to be processed. The business model used to be only food waste consumed but since many restaurants closed, the business shifted to a pilot project in a residential area (Cleantech no. 7).

> Our strategic partners are waste banks, so we cannot operate if the waste banks are not active. Since the activity of the waste banks is a physical activity, it was affected by the pandemic, and therefore it has also affected us (Cleantech no. 4).

After more than a year of operating under pandemic restrictions, startups have learned to cope and adapt. Some startups have diversified their customers (i.e., approached new customer segments), focused more on online services (i.e., held online consultations), or allowed their customers to adopt more technologies to support remote business operations.

> On the positive side, the pandemic has opened our minds to go into other sectors and not only [stay] in one sector (Cleantech no. 10).

> The impact of the pandemic is that more and more people are open to the idea that the use of technology can have more potential and that they can better monitor their activities every day without having to go to the field (Cleantech no. 1).

Challenges in Each Phase and Support Needed

The study divides the life of a startup into three main stages: formation, stability, and scaling. We asked startups to assess which stage they are currently in. We asked them to reflect on the challenges they faced in the different stages and the support needed to overcome these challenges. A summary of the responses can be found in Table 13.

Table 13: Challenges Faced by Cleantech Startups at Each Phase

Aspects of Challenges		Challenges in Each Phase			Support Needed
		Formation	Stability	Scaling	
Startup	Product	Challenges in research and development, sourcing components, manufacturing, and product testing	Product-market fit, marketing	n/a	• Product development research grant • Mentors, incubators, and accelerators to help validate the product and find the best product-market fit
	Funding	Grant, seed funding	Grant, investment	Investment	• Access to investors • Impact investment scheme
	Government	Lack of clear regulations to help the early stages	Lack of active regulations and/or policies to generate customer demand and allow startups' products to be implemented	n/a	• Consumer education • Incentive and disincentive scheme • Business-to-government agreements
	Founder and team capacity and talent	Difficulty in finding high-quality talent for core team	Increasing current talent and expanding the team	Increasing current talent and expanding the team	• Talent development • More responsive education
	Incubators and accelerators	Help product validation	Support to make more advanced developments	n/a	• More specialized incubators and accelerators
Sectoral	Market	Lack of public awareness of the cleantech sector	Difficulty in establishing market presence	Difficulty in tapping into new markets (new segments, new geographies)	• Consumer education • Incentives/disincentives • Cohesive regulatory system • Push from important stakeholders and decision makers
	Technology	n/a	Developing more advanced cleantech solutions	Lagging technology development compared to other countries	• Specialized incubators and accelerators • Push from important stakeholders and decision makers

n/a = not applicable.
Source: Authors.

Formation

In the formation stage, the most significant challenge mentioned by cleantech startups is product development. This ranges from R&D to sourcing components and manufacturing. Startups with a service offering need to continuously adjust and develop their main services.

> The challenge at this stage is that when you finalize the idea, you should not only make decisions after several attempts, but you really need to have iterations, so you don't have to go back to the initial stage (Cleantech no. 10).

Experimentation and iteration of ideas are commonplace in this phase, and therefore R&D capacity and resources are important. Access to incubators, accelerators, and mentors also help startups validate their product. In terms of capacity and resources for product development, funding and availability of talent are the next big challenges in the formation stage.

One informant argued that funding support is important in the formation stage to help teams to fully hone the potential of the product and the business model. However, funding support is especially scarce in the early stages because startups are considered risky, even more so for cleantech startups whose market is relatively small compared with other sectors. Angel investors can step in at this stage, but it is difficult for startups to access them. Therefore, grants are ideal.

> In the early stages, working capital is still lacking. In the initial stages, a grant is needed to enable the team to work, but at the same time, there is potential for abuse here, as some [startups] do not use the grant according to its [terms] (Cleantech no. 7).

> In the beginning, the most difficult aspect was to find investors, as not many believe in the potential of the technology, especially with a business model like ours, which is quite complicated for the waste sector (Cleantech no. 5).

Recruiting high-quality talent is particularly difficult in Indonesia during the formation stage because it is expensive. Fresh graduates with good capabilities prefer stable jobs. In general, however, there is a skills gap in the labor market, and the Indonesian workforce cannot meet the talent requirements of fast-advancing industries. The education sector and curriculum in Indonesia have not adapted to the evolving job market needs.

> In terms of human resources, it is also difficult because if you are looking for seniors, the pay is high. On the other hand, if you are looking for fresh graduates, most of them want to join a unicorn (Cleantech no. 1).

Navigating the early stages of the venture is also difficult due to lack of regulatory clarity in the cleantech sector. As mentioned, government regulations are still lacking, although some startups can benefit from operating in gray areas.

Stability

In the stability stage, the biggest challenge relates to the product and finding the right fit for the market. The challenges mentioned by startups not only relate to the startup's internal efforts to adjust the product to match customer needs but also to position the product through a branding strategy.

Broader stakeholders also play an important role in raising awareness of cleantech and growing and developing the market as a whole. These efforts include government incentives to generate customer demand, regulations to enforce better systems that allow startups' products to be implemented, and business-to-business or business-to-government agreements.

> The market is still not large, so it will take a long time to get [i.e., expand] the market. This insufficient market is also influenced by the low level of awareness. Support from the ecosystem to enlarge the market, namely, from the government, with the existence of waste management regulations that require people to be aware of the environment, makes it easy to convince the public and is quite helpful in enlarging the market. The existence of regulations for waste management and processing should also directly address the public, not just industry; as should the existence of incentives for people to carry out their obligations (Cleantech no. 1).

> Regarding constraints in terms of marketing, the ecosystem can help startups validate their products, as a place between the startups and those who need the product—customers, B2B, or business to government (Cleantech no. 7).

In the stability stage, establishing a market presence becomes the focus of startups. To develop a strong brand reputation, startups must already have a solid and sophisticated team that possesses business and technology expertise. However, their current talent was also mentioned as one of the challenges startups face. In this regard, two startups said that mentors, incubators, and accelerators could play an important role. One informant added that access to specialized incubators would also be beneficial for startups to make more advanced developments.

> In the stability stage, it's more about the value and the company so that the company can sustain and grow. The direction is more toward the organization; how to make a good corporate system so that every [part of the] organization is running in the same direction. So, the issue is on the organizational side, because the company itself is growing (Cleantech no. 9).

Issues from the formation stage (e.g., talent and funding) were also mentioned by startups for the stability stage. Funding challenges relate to the startups' ability to recruit new talent, improve technologies, and conduct business development. Recruiting new talent, which is also a factor in improving technologies and business development, has become a challenge due to a lack of quality talent, which is further constrained by a lack of funding.

> The current internal challenge is human resources, because now the focus is on application development. There are several application segments [for which] we are still looking for talent, and in the regions it is quite difficult to find talent. Most of our talent comes from Jakarta (Cleantech no. 5).

> There is a talent gap. This causes obstacles in data management and legality because there are few people. The reason for not increasing the number of workers is that funding is also an important problem at this stage (Cleantech no. 6).

Scaling

Funding and talent are the biggest challenges when startups are looking to grow and expand. Expenses increase as output is ramped up and need to be funded. Startups also need to fund ongoing research and development. As noted, the availability of finance, especially foreign investment, remains limited due to weak valuation mechanisms and little impact investment for cleantech.

> Funding is needed when there is a target for scale-up that cannot be covered by current structures such as self-funding or previous rounds. The goal to grow is not because we run out of funds, but we need [to get to] the next level (Cleantech no. 9).

> Funding from the grant side is already good enough because we already know what investors are looking for. However, on the investment side, we are still treated the same as an early stage [startup], so there are not many [investors] (Cleantech no. 1).

Startups also need to increase their talent, either by adding personnel or by increasing the capacity of existing staff. In terms of talent, startups expressed difficulty in finding talent that fits the needs of their current development trajectory. In this stage, achieving growth targets and improving management are priorities, so the focus of hiring has shifted somewhat from finding like-minded individuals with shared idealism, to professional staff. In terms of recruitment of recent graduates, enthusiasm for the cleantech sector, notably waste management, is relatively low compared with other industries. One startup mentioned that it offers volunteer work or internships to attract new talent.

In addition to new hires, efforts can also be made to improve the capacity of current employees. Team members could be expected to develop crucial skills for management and administration.

> Team members are increasingly required to improve management skills. We are starting to be neater in terms of target documentation and KPIs [key performance indicators]. We are also trying to make a system of OKR so that innovation does not get stuck on mediocre targets.[28] Therefore, we want to include people who already have managerial experience. Sometimes, social enterprises like us hire people who share the same vision, but now what we see [need] is more about background experience, we need professional people [with] more professional experience to develop this even more (Cleantech no. 2).

The startups we interviewed in this phase—or preparing for this phase—mentioned geographic expansion and product diversification as key challenges. In geographic expansion, regional governments become stakeholders, as they can influence their populations to adapt to the norms required to adopt cleantech innovation.

> In the scaling stage, for geographic expansion, it is necessary to adapt to the market system in the regions, so the role of local government is very important site by site because the government can most influence the community to be responsible for waste. Currently, people still burn rubbish in the open, throw garbage in rivers, and so on, so they don't see the value [of our services] (Cleantech no. 2).

For diversification, startups mentioned the importance of partners helping them educate people about their products.

Regardless of the path to scaling, some startups expected that the startup growth trajectory in cleantech would be slower than in other sectors. Limited access to foreign technologies has slowed domestic product development. Furthermore, despite alarming developments in environmental damage and climate change, government decision makers and other stakeholders are still too slow to act. This in turn has hindered the development of the cleantech market and related technologies.

---

[28] Objectives and key results is an approach to engage team members' perspectives and align them with determinable goals. It is used by Silicon Valley companies including Intel, Google, Twitter, and Spotify.

Access to technology is not as fast in Indonesia as it is for our competitors outside. The effect is that our products are slower [to develop] (Cleantech no. 6).

The supply from the ecosystem for greentech is not as competitive as in other sectors, so although we are very confident that greentech or startups in this field will grow [albeit slowly], the government and business actors will also gradually know that the environmental impact is getting worse because it will have an impact on their business, and they will need our services, but currently there are not many [who are aware] (Cleantech no. 7).

Recommendations

Extensive information was collected from both ecosystem players, including startups, in the four market segments. These sources of information (insights, perceptions, opinions) form the basis for general recommendations for all sectors, followed by specific recommendations for agritech, edtech, greentech, and healthtech.

8.1 All Sectors

Incubators and Accelerators

Expand the number of incubators and accelerators outside Java and Bali. Incubators and accelerators have emerged rapidly in Indonesia recently. However, most programs are in Java and Bali, resulting in an uneven distribution across the country. The government can provide incentives for more programs to be set up in other regions.

Improve the business aspects support offered by university incubators and accelerators. The landscape of programs is dominated by university programs due to support from the government. This results in a focus on the research and technology aspects of innovation with less focus on the business aspects. Improved support for business management and marketing can be provided by hiring more people with business experience to manage programs and act as mentors. Partnerships can be built between university incubators and private businesses, and between university research departments and private incubators and accelerators.

Link government funding to the performance of incubators and accelerators. Funding for programs should be based on the achievement of key performance indicators (KPI) to ensure that improved service is provided. KPIs can include, in part, the satisfaction of startup tenants. KPIs for advanced programs in Java and Bali should be different than for newer programs in other regions. In regions and sectors where incentives for private sector programs are weak, the government should come to the forefront.

Move to sustainable funding. Current schemes fund incubators and accelerators on an annual basis. (In the case of new budgetary constraints, such as those caused by the COVID-19 pandemic, the incubator and accelerator support programs were put on hold.) Therefore, there is a need to develop endowment funds specifically for long-term use by incubators and accelerators.

Programs should be more tailored. Incubator and accelerator programs should be better tailored to the specific needs of tenants, rather than providing general advice and support to all. Startup needs vary by sector and the stage of startup development.

The impact on development—and not strictly on the economy—should be valued. The human, social, and environmental impacts of startups can be better recognized and supported. Currently, programs play an important role in filtering startups for support and investment. When filtered only by economic criteria such as short-term returns, market traction, and user acquisition, tech startups in the four development sectors (agritech, edtech, greentech, and healthtech) receive less support and investment than e-commerce, fintech, and other popular sectors. In short, there is a need to move from an "economic only" paradigm to one that includes human, social, and environmental impacts.

Financing Institutions

There are a variety of financing sources in Indonesia. These include angel investors, venture capital funds, venture builders, large corporations (and their venture capital), and emerging crowdfunding platforms. Startups also receive grants from government and donors, as well as prize money from competitions. In addition to these external sources, internal funds such as the founders' savings and contributions from family and friends are also used in the early phase.

The potential supply of finance is not the problem—it is the mismatch between supply and demand. E-commerce and fintech are popular with investors, while the four sectors examined in this report are seen as riskier and less profitable. Perceptions are based in part on investors' lack of knowledge about these sectors. The attractiveness of the four sectors can be increased through awareness and success stories. The government and other ecosystem stakeholders can do this by highlighting the technological innovation and social impact of these sectors.

Create sector-specific outlook reports on the prospects of startups in the four sectors and get media attention. These reports could track current startup developments and raise the sectors' profiles. The reports would increase investor interest in these sectors. Regular updates could be provided online. The government or a startup industry association could set up a dashboard of news and developments. The government can lead the formation of forums, consortia, and institutions that bring together investors, industry players, and startups to create opportunities and generate investment in these sectors. Such activities would increase investor familiarity with these sectors and improve networking. Finally, media attention can be encouraged to raise awareness of the four sectors among traditional investors.

Spread investments more evenly across the regions. This would reduce the current concentration in Jakarta and the wider Java and Bali areas. There is a need for investment incentives—especially for angel investors and subsidiaries of state-owned enterprises (SoEs)—to become more involved in underserved areas. Through their offices across the country, SoE subsidiaries can offer corporate venture capital to startups. At the same time, initiatives to improve the local business ecosystems will help develop better startups that are attractive to investors.

Increase financial literacy for startups. Barriers to financing can be reduced through financial education and mentoring programs for startups. Startups can learn more about securing funding, the variety of potential sources, and the benefits and obligations associated with each type of funding.

Equity crowdfunding can be encouraged as a new source of funding for startups. ECF platforms are a nascent investment channel in Indonesia that is still unknown to most startups. However, they have the potential to serve as an important potential source of funding, especially in the very early stages.

Provide more funding for early-stage startups. Many informants across all four sectors noted a lack of funding for startups in the early stages. Early in their development, startups are engaged in resource-consuming activities such as research, prototyping, and testing, which require funding at a time when the startup is not yet generating revenue. Funding is especially scarce for startups in the four sectors because they are not well known and are perceived to be high risk. More funding options at the early stages to provide working capital would help startups overcome the "valley of death."

Government Programs

The government offers a variety of support programs, which are implemented by different ministries. The most important programs are provided by the Ministry of Education, Culture, Research and Technology; the Ministry of Information and Communication Technology; and the Ministry of Industry. In addition, Kedaireka was launched at the end of 2020 to provide matching funds for university startups that have secured other funds.

The government can facilitate consultations and networking between startups, other businesses, and financial institutions. Many current government programs focus only on organizing events, such as demo days and program launches. While these events are good for promotional purposes, follow-up activities are even more important to truly foster collaboration between players. Therefore, the government should hold coordination meetings and consultations after the events to bring startups closer to other businesses, financing institutions, and important stakeholders in the ecosystem. Networks of startups and stakeholders can be established to ensure ongoing and continuous dialogue.

Access procedures for government programs can be streamlined through the use of digital technology. Digital transformation is a major theme of the National Medium-Term Development Plan (RPJMN) 2020–2024, so it is important to digitalize the accountability process for programs that support startups. For example, administrative and financial reports can be submitted in soft copy. Complicated administrative and financial reports are challenging and time-consuming for startups.

Improve the use (and reporting requirements) of government grants. For example, startups tend to use government grants for hardware purchases because this is more readily accepted in reporting procedures, whereas soft inputs such as market research and product validation, while necessary, are not as readily accepted as grant expenditures.

The government can educate consumers about startups' products and services (and help startups do so). Such education would make people more open to using the new technologies offered by startups. This is especially true in the agriculture sector, where farmers are reluctant to embrace new technologies for various reasons (risk aversion, low digital literacy, aging). Introducing startups to potential customers at trade shows and events can help them learn about the problems people and businesses face and explain their solutions.[29] In agriculture, extension officers can facilitate interaction between startups and farmers or other customers. The media can also play a role in raising public awareness about the use of new products and technologies.

Improve the coverage and quality of digital (and other) infrastructure. Many startup products and services use the internet. Therefore, the government can provide sufficient infrastructure throughout the country, particularly outside Java and the big cities. To do this, it must collaborate with local government. For example, if the central government wants to build base transceiver stations,

---

[29] Compared with marketing, consumer education focuses more on the problem the product will solve and on expert opinion about its value. It is not simply about selling the product, but explaining to the consumer the bigger issues and the context surrounding the product (Craig 2015).

the local government could expedite land acquisition and permit processing. Also, maintenance costs for base transceiver stations are high, as spare parts are often stolen or vandalized. Therefore, the local government could also put in place measures to reduce these incidents. The government can also provide incentives for internet service providers to offer their services throughout the country. Moreover, digital infrastructure should be complemented by other infrastructure such as electricity, roads, and water supply, to support overall economic activity.

The Government as an Enabler in the Startup Ecosystem

The government can act as an enabler to ensure that policies and regulations support the functions of stakeholders in the ecosystem for the benefit of startups. The following recommendations relate specifically to the government as an enabler.

Provide alternative sources of funding for local venture capital firms. Financial Services Authority Regulation No. 35/2015 allows and encourages local VCs (that invest mainly in SMEs) to establish venture funds and invite other investors to contribute. However, most local VCs would not set up such a fund because of the high risk. In this context, the government could explore the establishment of venture funds under a public–private partnership model, with both the government and private VC contributing. Another source could be the Sovereign Wealth Fund, which the government recently launched.

Improve licensing, regulation, and intellectual property rights. Business regulation, including licenses and permits (i.e., ease of doing business) can be improved, including for enterprises receiving foreign investment. More importantly, procedures for filing intellectual property applications (i.e., patents) can be streamlined, which currently involve long delays. Intellectual property is crucial because many investors will only fund startups whose innovations are protected. Moreover, Assegaf (2020) highlighted that Singapore is favorable for investment because it has a high reputation for enforcing contracts. In the World Bank's Ease of Doing Business 2019, Singapore is ranked number 1 in contract enforcement, while Indonesia is ranked 139th.

Experiment with regulatory sandboxes. A sandbox has been created for fintech. The Ministry of Information and Communication Technology will assess the application of this method in other sectors. Healthtech could be given priority with efforts later extended to agritech, edtech, and greentech.

Mechanisms to exit equity from a startup can be improved. This includes the rate at which capital gains are taxed, which is currently 25%, while in Singapore it is zero. An easier exit could encourage more investment in startups.[30] Easier exit procedures and no capital gains tax could explain why Indonesian startups are funded in Singapore.

Foster better digital infrastructure. Many tech startups rely on the internet to attract customers and deliver their services. Therefore, improving digital infrastructure will help almost all startups. The recently approved Master Plan for Digital Industry, 2023–2045, is likely to provide significant support to the ecosystem.

8.2   Sector Recommendations

The following recommendations relate to the four market segments that are the focus of the study: agritech, edtech, greentech, and healthtech. A common theme is that knowledge of these areas needs to be improved to ensure greater support from funders—who see these areas as risky because they do not understand them. Also, support from ecosystem planners will be most effective when it is tailored to the specific characteristics of each sector and draws on sector expertise to provide guidance and mentorship.

Agritech

Improve local government support to link startups with farmers. Agritech startups can benefit from the support of local government to link them with farmers and other players. By getting closer to the sector, startups can better understand farmers' needs and the farming context. Programs like Digital Village and Millennial Farmers are worth adopting as they bring technology closer to agriculture and farm youth. Agriculture extension workers who are open to innovation and technology can encourage farmers to adopt the technologies offered by startups. Educating farmers can start with educating extension workers and hiring workers who are knowledgeable about innovation and technology.

Nurture skilled talent in agriculture. To encourage talent to use agritech in farms, the curriculum at vocational schools under provincial authority can be modified to include technology subjects, and teachers should be trained to teach these subjects.

Increase investment in farms. Bank officers can be trained to understand tech-based products and services so that banks are more willing to lend to farmers to purchase the innovations of startups. Moreover, the current ceiling on KUR, the farm credit program, could be increased or complemented with other loan sources to cover the cost of startups' products.

---

[30]   In addition to equity participation, Article 2 of OJK Regulation No. 35/2015 provides that VC may finance startups with (i) quasi-equity participation, (ii) financing through the purchase of bonds, and (iii) financing of productive business.

Boost demand through policies to protect the environment and combat climate change. This will encourage sustainable agriculture and increase demand for solutions from agritech and greentech startups.

Edtech

Increase media coverage of edtech performance and benefits to attract more investors. The education and training sector is still not considered attractive to investors and users compared with fintech and e-commerce. Edtech startups should "sell" themselves better and highlight their social impacts to impact investors. Involving youth in edtech events would strengthen the understanding of how important edtech is for the education of the next generation.

Explore the use of technology, including edtech products, to improve the quality of education. There is great potential to optimize technology to increase enthusiasm and improve learning processes and outcomes. Greater use and experimentation of edtech products should be encouraged by education managers in schools, colleges, and universities. Edtech startups should do their part by helping school authorities and teachers improve the quality of teaching and learning.

Improve teachers' awareness and skills in using digital technology. Effective use of digital technologies should be included in teacher training. This will encourage teachers to use edtech in the classroom. It is important that edtech enterprises develop software that is friendly to teachers, even among boomers and Gen X who are less tech-savvy than younger people. This friendly application will spark teachers' enthusiasm and increase their willingness to use it to complement traditional teaching methods. Upskilling teachers, especially those outside Java and Bali, in the use of edtech (or hiring teachers with these skills) will increase demand for edtech startups' products and services in classrooms.

Use edtech to deliver public training programs. Before the pandemic, the government spent generously on in-person (offline) training. However, during the pandemic, all in-person training was paused. The Kartu Prakerja program was introduced and revolutionized the way training was delivered by allowing trainees to use vouchers to select the training they needed. The program spurred demand for training and learning management systems provided by edtech. Future government training activities can follow the Kartu Prakerja method, in which the government conducts training in partnership with edtech startups, either fully online or in hybrid form.

Improve internet access at the school level. The pandemic has shown how the internet can be used for education. However, unequal internet access across the country has created disparity in students' ability to learn from home. Students have gone back to school and the use of the internet and digital technologies in school should be expanded. The government can ensure that all schools have internet access, allowing them to use the products and services of edtech startups.

Healthtech

Encourage incubators and the use of mentors who specialize specifically in healthtech. Due to the highly regulated and sensitive nature of the health-care sector, startups require sector-specific assistance. Mentorship that combines business, tech, and health can be very helpful, as can dedicated rather than generic incubator and accelerator programs. Support can also extend to product registration, as the process of completing market authorization and patenting intellectual property rights for healthtech can take months and sometimes years. Some healthtech startups that have more initial capital can hire a consultant to tackle these issues, while others cannot. Hence, health-specific incubation and mentoring are needed.

Introducing healthtech to early adopters can increase demand. The pandemic has increased the pace of healthtech innovation and the range of new solutions. The Ministry of Health worked closely with the health-care industry and startups under COVID-19 collaboration schemes. This collaboration has helped introduce the products and services of some healthtech startups to customers. Greater government support in linking healthtech startups with early adopters (e.g., hospitals, clinics, health-care professionals, patients) allows startups to expand their customer base and better understand the problems for which solutions are needed.

Promote disruption and innovation to transform the health-care sector. The health sector is perceived by startups and other players as unable or unwilling to absorb innovative solutions and to do so quickly. Innovation is not disrupting health care like other sectors. To accelerate technology adoption, key players— governments, end users, health-care providers, insurance companies, and pharmaceutical firms—can be educated on how innovation and technology can transform the sector.

Emphasize promotive and preventive solutions—alongside curative ones. Current practice focuses on curative solutions, an approach that is deeply rooted in Indonesia's health sector. Transforming the health-care industry means shifting to greater emphasis on promotive and preventive solutions. Healthtech startups can offer such solutions.

Ensure interoperability of health data while protecting patient privacy. The draft Law on Personal Data Protection may have a major impact on electronic medical records and health information exchange, services that healthtech solutions require. Therefore, it is essential to regulate electronic medical records as shareable data while protecting patient privacy. Nuanced policies are needed to ensure that privacy and data interoperability are equally recognized as critical in the health-care industry.

Cleantech Sector and Cleantech Startups

Provide cleantech-specific incubators and accelerators. Given the techno-specific nature of the sector, startups need incubators and accelerators, and associated mentors who can provide a deep understanding of cleantech and related markets. Some foreign incubators and accelerators currently provide cleantech-specific guidance, but Indonesian startups will need to compete in regional and global competitions to access them.

Develop networks and platforms to consolidate cleantech expertise—domestically and abroad. Sector-specific platforms are needed to bring together cleantech experts and their networks from various cleantech subsectors. Cleantech leaders from developed markets could also be courted. Although the cleantech sector in Indonesia is just emerging, there are already prominent figures in Indonesia working on environmental sustainability and climate change. Stakeholders in the startup ecosystem could enlist these figures for mentorship. Forming a cleantech network or platform is also an option. Startups and sector leaders could share knowledge in a structured or unstructured setting. Also, global cleantech leaders or organizations could be invited to Indonesia to form joint-venture incubation and accelerator programs with local partners.

Promote impact investments in cleantech. The low level of funding for cleantech startups could be reversed through impact investments. Impact investing is characterized by the intention to create positive social and environmental impact in exchange for a financial return that can be below the market rate. Impact investment is still relatively unknown among local investors. To encourage such investment, the government could engage financing institutions and large firms to invest in greentech by forming business partnerships with startups to show proof of financial viability. At the same time, barriers to the flow of foreign impact investment should be eased to support cleantech startups.

Demonstrate the social value of greentech and other impact investments. To further develop the impact investment ecosystem, methods can be devised to measure and publicize the social value of impact investments and their financial performance. Success stories could be disseminated to inspire stakeholders to invest. Similarly, cleantech and other social entrepreneurs should be made aware of what aspects to look for when evaluating an impact investment proposal. Tax incentives could be created for investors and startups in this sector.

Enforce environmental regulations to stimulate demand for greentech. Indonesia already has regulations in place to promote the use of environmentally friendly products and minimize the use of harmful products. However, they are not complemented by clear implementation guidelines and accountability measures. It is therefore important to provide these so that regulations can be enforced and so that demand for of cleantech startups can be stimulated.

Ensure that decentralization policies are cohesive. Overlapping authority under decentralization policies pose a challenge for cleantech. Startups operating at the local level must deal with both local authorities and the central government, which govern the energy sector. Waste management is a regional responsibility, and regulations and policies can vary from region to region. The growth of cleantech startups in different regions can vary greatly depending on the regulatory environment and regional political will.

Clear agency access points for greentech startups are needed at both the national and regional levels. Regional–national and regional–regional differences in regulations, policies, and agencies need to be mediated if regulations are difficult to change at the national level. Agency entry points should allow startups to access both national and regional agencies. This will allow startups to have a more continuous engagement process with all levels of government.

Create a national sector road map for greentech. This would bridge regional differences in regulations and policies for the greentech sector and its subsectors, and offer policy guidance to regional governments to align their policies with those at the national level. A model for the road map could be the Sustainable Development Goals (SDG) Action Plan, which exists at the national level and is supported by SDG regional actional plans from provincial governments. Since the implementation of the SDGs in Indonesia is both top–down and bottom–up, this could provide an opportunity to bridge local and national initiatives, involve startups in drafting of regulations, and invite them to be partners in implementing and achieving the SDGs in greentech.

Appendix
Government Startup Support Programs

Program	Ministry	Start Year	Target	Type of Support Provided
Perusahaan Pemula Berbasis Teknologi (PPBT)	Ministry of Education, Culture, Research and Technology[a]	2013	Startups scaled up to Advanced Tech-Based Startup Grant Program (Perusahaan Lanjut Berbasis Teknologi [PLBT])	Funding of Rp100 million–Rp500 million provided through incubation program for a maximum of 2 years to commercialize the products
Hub.ID	Ministry of Communication and Information Technology	2014	Startups to be matched with investors and connected with corporate and government partners	Acceleration program to intensify growth; 2-day summit to link with global venture capitalists and business partners; and ecosystem to collaborate and search for new opportunities
Calon Perusahaan Pemula Berbasis Teknologi (CPPBT)	Ministry of Education, Culture, Research and Technology[a]	2016	Pre-startups scaled up to enter the PPBT program	Incubation consisting of team development and product development, 1 year
1000 Startups Digital Program	Ministry of Communication and Information Technology	2016	Early-stage startups in agriculture, health, education, tourism, logistics, maritime	Incubation for 3–6 months consisting of (i) discussion with stakeholders, (ii) bootcamp to develop minimum viable product, and (iii) one-on-one mentoring
Baparekraf for Startup (BEKUP) Academy	Ministry of Tourism and Creative Economy/ Tourism and Creative Economy Agency	2016	Early-stage startups that already have a minimum viable product	Incubation program consisting of (i) 2-day bootcamp in each large city focused on designing products that could help solve creative and/or social challenges at the local level; (ii) one-on-one mentoring; and (iii) facilitating startups' pitching sessions to VCs, corporate partners, and relevant government stakeholders In general, BEKUP has been held in around 17 big cities across Indonesia. During 2020, BEKUP was held in Jakarta, Surabaya, Bali, Medan, and Makassar.
E-Commerce Roadmap (Presidential Regulation 74/2017)	Ministry of Trade	2017	Ecommerce, SMEs, startups, and logistics	A steering committee of various relevant ministries and technical assistance formulating government regulations and ministerial regulations for e-commerce

continued on next page

Table *continued*

Program	Ministry	Start Year	Target	Type of Support Provided
Startup4industry Program	Ministry of Industry	2018	Startups that already have a minimum viable product	(i) Problem-solving competition to curate startup participants; (ii) Techlink matching activity between startups and larger businesses; and (iii) solution discussion by matching tech startups and problem owners and involving other stakeholders
Next Indonesian Unicorn	Ministry of Communication and Information Technology	2018	Later-stage startups in logistics, e-commerce, fintech, media and advertising, healthtech, edtech, SaaS	Facilitate contacts between startups and Series B investors, both locally and internationally, through one-on-one meetings and networking dinners
Startup Studio Indonesia	Ministry of Communication and Information Technology	2020	Startups in agriculture, health, education, tourism, logistics, and maritime sectors that have reached product market-fit stage	Intensive acceleration program for around 1.5 months, consisting of (i) business skills development and branding; and (ii) facilitating access to seed/pre-series A/series A investors
Kedaireka	Ministry of Education, Culture, Research and Technology	2020	Lecturers and students in higher education collaborate with businesses registered on the Kedaireka platform	Matching funds for collaborative projects with the business and upon approval of the submitted proposal by the Kedaireka board
BEKUP Mentor Training Program	Ministry of Tourism and Creative Economy/Tourism and Creative Economy Agency	2021	Startup enthusiasts, founders, and tech and business experts with minimum 2 years of experience in a managerial position	Upskilling individuals to act as mentors for startups through various activities such as workshops, consultations, and case simulations

SaaS = Software-as-a-Service, SMEs = small and medium-sized enterprises.
[a] Now provided through the National Research and Innovation Agency. The program was subsumed under Startup Inovasi Indonesia in 2020, which was later replaced by Program Pendanaan Perusahaan Pemula Berbasis Riset (PPBR) at the end of 2021.
Source: Authors.

References

Adelayanti, N. 2020. Regulatory Sandbox: Supporting Digital Health Innovations in the New Habit of Adaptation Era. Universitas Gadjah Mada.

Aldila, N. 2019. Amvesindo: Gerak PMV Masih Terganjal Pajak. *Bisnis.com*. Jakarta.

Alpha JWC Ventures. 2022. Early Startup Funding Stages: Explained from Seed to IPO.

ANGIN. 2020. Investing in Impact in Indonesia.

Appaya, S. and M. Haji. 2020. Four Years and Counting: What We've Learned from Regulatory Sandboxes. World Bank Blogs.

Assegaf, A. F. 2020. Kenapa Start Up Indonesia Beramai-ramai Pindah ke Singapura?. Hukum Online.com.

Bachtiar, P. P., R. A. Diningrat, A. Z. D. Kusuma, R. A. Izzati, and A. Diandra. 2020. Who Is Digital Economy for? Toward an Inclusive Digital Economy in Indonesia. SMERU Research Institute.

Bachtiar, P. P., H. W. Sawiji, and P. Vandenberg. 2022. City-Level Tech Startup Ecosystems and Talent Development in Indonesia. ADB Brief No. 228. Manila: ADB.

Baraldi, E. and M. I. Havenvid. 2016. Identifying New Dimensions of Business Incubation: A Multi-Level Analysis of Karolinska Institute's Incubation System. *Technovation*. 50–51. pp. 53–68.

Batunanggar, S. 2019. Fintech Development and Regulatory Frameworks in Indonesia. *ADBI Working Paper Series*. No. 1014. Tokyo: Asian Development Bank Institute.

BKPM. 2017. Penanaman Modal Asing di Indonesia. Jakarta.

Brillyanes, S. and B. A. Samira. 2019. Building Startups: The Design Elements of Startup Accelerators in Indonesia. *Eurasia: Economics & Business*. 8 (26). pp. 44–51.

Bruneel, J., T. Ratinho, B. Clarysse, and A. Groen. 2012. The Evolution of Business Incubators: Comparing Demand and Supply of Business Incubation Services Across Different Incubator Generations. *Technovation*. 32 (2). pp. 110–121.

Burhan, F. A. 2021. Kominfo Kaji Perluas Sandbox untuk Startup Fintech hingga Kesehatan. Katadata. Jakarta.

Caprotti, F. 2016. Defining a New Sector in the Green Economy: Tracking the Techno-Cultural Emergence of the Cleantech Sector, 1990–2010. *Technology in Society.* 46 (June). pp. 80–89.

Cekindo Editorial Team. 2022. Capital Gains Tax Indonesia: A Guide to Accounting and Tax Reporting. Jakarta.

Chen, C. C. 2020. Regulatory Sandboxes in the UK and Singapore: A Preliminary Survey. *SSRN Electronic Journal.* pp. 1–22.

Craig, W. 2015. Don't Market to Your Customers; Educate Them Instead. *Forbes.*

Deloitte. 2018. A Journey through the FCA Regulatory Sandbox. Deloitte LLP.

Directorate of Junior High School, Ministry of Education and Culture. 2021. Program Direktorat: Pembinaan Satuan Pendidikan Kerjasama. Jakarta.

Eka, R. 2020. Startup Report 2019: Scaling Through Technology Democratization. *DailySocial.*

_____. 2022. Startup Report 2021 (and Q1 2022). *DailySocial.*

Etzkowitz, H., J. M. C. De Mello, and M. Almeida. 2005. Towards "Meta-Innovation" in Brazil: The Evolution of the Incubator and the Emergence of a Triple Helix. *Research Policy.* 34 (4). pp. 411–424.

Firdaus, F. 2021. Pandu Sjahrir Tegaskan IPO Bukalapak Bukan Strategi Exit Investor. *Bisnis.com.* Jakarta.

Gozali, L., M. Masrom, T. Y. M. Zagloel, and H. N. Haron. 2015. A Framework of Successful Business Incubators for Indonesian Public Universities. *The Asian Journal of Technology Management.* 8 (2). pp. 120–134.

Greenhouse Team. 2021. The Pros and Cons of Running a Startup in Indonesia in 2021.

Gunawan, A. 2020. Produk Dana Ventura, Sumber Dana Baru Bagi Industri Modal Ventura. *Bisnis.com.* Jakarta.

Gusman, H. 2018. Pasang Surut Investasi Asing Tergantung Rezim yang Berkuasa. *Tirto.id.* Jakarta.

Haliding, S. 2018. Outlook Modal Ventura dan Startup 2018. *Investor.id.* Jakarta.

Hana, O. DB. 2017. Ternyata Ini Sumber Pendanaan Modal Ventura. *Bisnis.com.* Jakarta.

References

Harususilo, Y. E. 2022. Ditjen Dikti Luncurkan 7 Program Ekosistem Kedaireka. *Kompas.com*. Jakarta.

Hecht, J. 2017. Are You Running a Startup or Small Business? What's the Difference?. *Forbes.com*.

Hendayana, Y. 2021. Kedaireka dan Matching Fund untuk Akselerasi Reka Cipta Perguruan Tinggi dan DUDI. Directorate General of Higher Education, Ministry of Education and Culture. Jakarta.

Ika, S. 2017. Warta Fiskal. *Badan Kebijakan Fiskal*. 52.

Indeed Editorial Team. 2021. How Startup Funding Works and the 8 Startup Funding Stages. *Indeed.com*.

Indonesian Association of Business Incubators. 2020. Daftar Inkubator Bisnis di Indonesia. Jakarta.

Investor.id. 2015. OJK Perluas Kegiatan Usaha Perusahaan Modal Ventura. Jakarta.

Iras.Gov.Sg. 2022. Inland Revenue Authority of Singapore.

Jensen, F., H. Lööf, and A. Stephan. 2020. New Ventures in Cleantech: Opportunities, Capabilities and Innovation Outcomes. *Business Strategy and the Environment*. 29 (3). pp. 902–917.

Kirk, R. 2021. What Is a Startup Ecosystem. *LinkedIn*.

Kompas.com. 2019. Menumbuhkan "Startup" Kampus lewat "CPPBT Boot Camp 2019." Jakarta.

Lenggogeni, R. and E. K. Subiakto. 2020. Venture Capital Investment in Indonesia: Market and Regulatory Overview. *Thomson Reuters Practical Law*.

Leow, A. 2020. Agri-Food Sandbox, Product Design Space among Government's New Innovation Ideas. *The Business Times*.

Manurung, M. Y. 2018. 20 Tahun Reformasi: Tapak Tilas Sejarah Startup Indonesia. *Tempo.co*.

Paul Hype Page & Co. 2022. How to Register a Company in Indonesia?.

Putera, P. A. W. and B. Tang. 2020. *Indonesia Agritech Report 2020: Startups, Investors, and Outlook*. Jakarta: Compasslist.

Ratinho, T. and E. Henriques. 2010. The Role of Science Parks and Business Incubators in Converging Countries: Evidence from Portugal. *Technovation*. 30 (4). pp. 278–290.

Rayda, N. 2022. Pushing the Boundaries of Innovation: How 9 Indonesia Start-ups Become Unicorns during the Pandemic. *Channel News Asia*.

Rice, M. P. 2002. Co-Production of Business Assistance in Business Incubators: An Exploratory Study. *Journal of Business Venturing*. 17 (2). pp.163–187.

Rosenberg, M. 2021. What's Deep Tech and Why Should You Care?. *LinkedIn*.

Rosser, A. and M. Fahmi. 2016. The Political Economy of Teacher Management in Decentralized Indonesia. World Bank Group.

Ryza, P. 2020. Indonesia's Agritech to Develop Progressively. *DailySocial*.

Simpson, L. 2020. Sandboxes: Our Approach to Systemic Experimentation. *EdTech Hub*.

Sinamo, A. 2019. Menantikan Bangkitnya Modal Ventura Indonesia. *Indonesiana.id*.

Spender, J., V. Corvello, M. Grimaldi, and P. Rippa. 2017. Startups and Open Innovation: A Review of the Literature. *European Journal of Innovation Management*. 20 (1). pp. 4-30.

The GAIN. 2022. 5 Important Stages to Build a Successful Startup.

Vandenberg, P., A. Hampel-Milagrosa, and M. Helble. 2020. Financing of Tech Startups in Selected Asian Countries. *ADBI Working Paper Series*. No. 1115. Tokyo: ADB Institute.

Wahyudi, S. I. N. A. 2021. Investasi Asing di KEK Dibuka untuk Sektor Pendidikan. *Bisnis Indonesia*. Jakarta.

Wang, J. 2021. How Does a Deep Tech Startup Differ From a "Normal" Startup? *Creative Ventures*.

Webb, K., R. Cruz, and P. R. Walsh. 2017. A Comparative Review of the Role of Markets and Institutions in Sustaining Innovation in Cleantech: A Critical Mass Approach. *International Journal of Innovation and Sustainable Development*. 11 (2–3). pp. 149–169.

Wise, S. and D. Valliere. 2014. The Impact on Management Experience on the Performance of Startups within Accelerators. *Journal of Private Equity*. 18 (1). pp. 9–19.

World Bank. 2020a. EdTech in Indonesia : Ready for Take-off?. Washington, DC.

_____. 2020b. Doing Business 2020: Comparing Business Regulation in 190 Economies. Economy Profile Indonesia. Washington, DC.

_____. 2020c. Doing Business 2020: Comparing Business Regulation in 190 Economies. Economy Profile Singapore. Washington, DC.

Wymer, S. A. and E. A. Regan. 2005. Factors Influencing E-commerce Adoption and Use by Small and Medium Businesses. *Electronic Markets*. 15 (4).

www.ingramcontent.com/pod-product-compliance
Lightning Source LLC
Chambersburg PA
CBHW050044220326
41599CB00045B/7279

9 789292 701581